Satanism and Demonology

Also by Lionel and Patricia Fanthorpe

Oak Island
The World's Greatest Unsolved Mysteries
The World's Most Mysterious People
The World's Most Mysterious Places
Mysteries of the Bible
Death: The Final Mystery
The World's Most Mysterious Objects
The World's Most Mysterious Murders
Unsolved Mysteries of the Sea
Mysteries and Secrets of the Templars
The World's Most Mysterious Castles
Mysteries and Secrets of the Masons
Mysteries and Secrets of Voodoo, Santeria, and Obeah
Mysteries of Secrets of Time
Secrets of the World's Undiscovered Treasures
The Big Book of Mysteries

Lionel and Patricia Fanthorpe

Satanism and Demonology

DUNDURN PRESS
TORONTO

Copyright © Lionel and Patricia Fanthorpe, 2011

All rights reserved. No part of this publication may be reproduced, stored in a retrieval system, or transmitted in any form or by any means, electronic, mechanical, photocopying, recording, or otherwise (except for brief passages for purposes of review) without the prior permission of Dundurn Press. Permission to photocopy should be requested from Access Copyright.

Editor: Allison Hirst
Design: Courtney Horner
Printer: Marquis

Library and Archives Canada Cataloguing in Publication

Fanthorpe, Patricia
   Satanism and demonology : mysteries and secrets / Patricia and Lionel Fanthorpe.

Includes bibliographical references and index.
ISBN 978-1-55488-854-2

   1. Satanism. 2. Devil. I. Fanthorpe, R. Lionel II. Title.

BF1548.F35 2011   133.4'22   C2010-907726-1

1   2   3   4   5   15   14   13   12   11

We acknowledge the support of the **Canada Council for the Arts** and the **Ontario Arts Council** for our publishing program. We also acknowledge the financial support of the **Government of Canada** through the **Canada Book Fund** and **Livres Canada Books**, and the **Government of Ontario** through the **Ontario Book Publishers Tax Credit** program, and the **Ontario Media Development Corporation**.

Care has been taken to trace the ownership of copyright material used in this book. The author and the publisher welcome any information enabling them to rectify any references or credits in subsequent editions.

J. Kirk Howard, President

www.dundurn.com

All images are courtesy of the authors from their private collection.
Back cover image: *"Satan, King of Hell."* Front cover image: *"Lucifer Cast Out."* Both engravings by Gustave Doré.

Dundurn Press	Gazelle Book Services Limited	Dundurn Press
3 Church Street, Suite 500	White Cross Mills	2250 Military Road
Toronto, Ontario, Canada	High Town, Lancaster, England	Tonawanda, NY
M5E 1M2	LA1 4XS	U.S.A. 14150

This book is dedicated to all the kind, generous, loving, unselfish, and caring people all over the world who oppose evil by doing good.

Contents

	Foreword by Canon Stanley Mogford, M.A.	9
	Introduction	13
1	What Is Satanism?	15
2	The Early History of Satanism	24
3	Satanism in the Middle East	35
4	Satanism in Ancient Egypt	44
5	Satanism in the Dark Ages	57
6	Medieval Satanism	72
7	Renaissance Satanism	87
8	Contemporary Satanism	104
9	Satan in the Abrahamic Religions	117
10	The Identity, Character, and Nature of Satan	134
11	Satanic Worship and Ritual	145
12	Satanic Sex Magic	160
13	The Seventy-Two Solomonic Demons	170
14	Satanism in Salem	185
15	Demon Reports: A Survey	197
16	The Church of Satan and Other Satanic Groups	211
17	Does Satan Exist?	219
	Bibliography	225

FOREWORD

For more than twenty years now it has been my privilege to write a foreword to many of the books written by Patricia and Lionel Fanthorpe. This one for the first time I do with a somewhat heavy heart, not because of the book, which, as always with the Fanthorpes, is meticulously researched and carefully written. What daunts my pen is the subject matter of the book.

Satan and I have never existed for each other. The late C.S. Lewis, in his book *The Screwtape Letters*, relates how Screwtape advises Wormwood, one of the young devil nephews, how best to do maximum damage to the world around him. In one letter his advice is to go round persuading everyone he meets that Satan really doesn't exist, is, in fact, simply an invention from the long-distant past. Thus, relieved of any fear of consequences, sinners may feel free to do any wicked act that appeals to them. Well! Wormwood certainly succeeded with me. I have never been able to believe in Satan as a person, or any of his satanic angels, or any part of the paraphernalia that goes with them. The satanic world has never existed for me nor will it ever, unless of course I have it all wrong and I eventually end up in his everlasting company!

However, it doesn't follow that, having no belief in Satan, I have no concept of evil. No one who has lived through two world wars, as people of my generation have, having lost friends on the battlefield or blasted to death in their own homes, can do other than shudder at the evil that set into motion such mass global slaughter. Those who were present at the liberation of concentration camps, such as Belsen or Dachau, will never get over the stench of evil revealed in those camps.

Evil is a reality. It always has been and, sadly, no doubt we shall never be free of it. Its origins, to our shame, may be not with Satan, but from within the human heart. It might be more comforting to lay the burden on some outside demonic presence but we may have to bear the responsibility for ourselves.

Satan as an entity some of us can't come to terms with but satanic evil we can. However, life is not all doom and gloom. Evil doesn't consume life. It cheers the heart to remember that not all that comes from the heart is evil. There also comes the glory of real goodness. Human nature we know sometimes produces monsters; it also produces angels. Where the few inflict evil after evil on the world, others spread goodness, compassion, kindliness, and self-sacrifice that sweeten life for everyone around them.

That having been said, whatever I may believe or you may believe, is not the end of it. The fact remains that many have had, and still have, an unshakeable belief in Satan and his angel demons. Millions do to this day and countless millions have been devil conscious all down the centuries and all over the world. Probably many will go on believing in the satanic world until the end of time. What the Fanthorpes have done is to research those beliefs in all their infinite variety. They have explored all ages and examined many different countries. It must have been a massive undertaking.

Satan has been shown to have many names and appear in many guises. Every nation seems to have feared him and the research has covered the great variety of ways people devised to protect themselves from him, defending their health, their crops, and their families. Some took a different stance. Oscar Wilde once said that the only thing he couldn't resist was temptation. Where people could not resist the devil, they joined him. They went so far as to worship him, daring even to conjure up his presence. It seems, even to this day, some still do.

The work involved in researching this book would leave most of us hopelessly defeated. The Fanthorpes seem inexhaustible in their studies. What they themselves believe about Satan and Satanism, if they believe in any of it at all, I don't know. What I do know, and all who read the book will feel the same, is that they have researched widely, and fairly, and without judgement or prejudice as they always do. I long for the day when the Fanthorpes, kindly, generous friends as they always are, will be commissioned to write not about the abnormalities of the world, but about its goodness. Devils have their fascination but so have Saints. Where does real goodness come from? Hopefully, some day, while they still have their gifts and energy, they will write of those who by the grace and beauty of their lives enriched the world of their generation. Evil has a horrible fascination. Goodness will always overcome it.

Canon Stanley Mogford,
M.A., *Cardiff, Wales, 2010*

Introduction

This research and analysis of Satanism and demonology begins by asking what Satanism is. How can we define and explain it? What is understood by demonology?

The best way to find out the real nature of a thing is to go back to its origins, to ask how it started and what it was like in the past. An examination of prehistoric deities and cave paintings of half-animal, half-human figures suggests that the earliest religions may have been something akin to shamanism. How far back does the idea of the very ancient nature spirit Pan take the research into the origins of Satanism?

The inhabitants of the ancient Middle East — Canaanites, Midianites, Persians, Philistines, and others — believed in numerous strange deities such as Melqart, Hadad, and Astarte. Some of them were good, others evil. What contribution did they make to the origins of Satanism? Moloch was a particularly satanic deity!

The mysterious animal-headed gods of ancient Egypt included Set, who was at various times in Egyptian history regarded as evil. What contribution did belief in him make to the development of Satanism and demonology? Apep was also an evil god in ancient Egypt. Another fiercely evil Egyptian demon-god was Shesmu, who tore off the heads of his victims and crushed their skulls like grapes in a wine press.

The Dark Ages, Medieval times, and the Renaissance had more than their fair share of witchcraft and black magic, all of which led people back to the belief that Satan and his demon hordes were responsible for most misfortunes and that evil wizards and witches were on his side. The strange witchcraft hysteria at Salem at the end of the seventeenth century is dealt with separately and in detail.

Satanism is examined closely in the light of the great Abrahamic religions, all of which offer protections against the forces of evil.

No assessment of Satanism and demonology would be complete without a survey of the sexual elements which are a major part of most satanic rituals. It was also felt useful to describe in detail the characteristics of the seventy-two demons imprisoned by Solomon and listed in the grimoires, as well as to give samples from a broad survey of contemporary reports of sightings of evil entities. The Church of Satan and other groups of Satanists are described in detail, and, finally, an attempt is made to answer the ultimate questions: Does Satan exist? and What sort of being is he?

A Special Note: The authors are, as always, deeply grateful to Canon Mogford for contributing the foreword. It is a great honour to have his support. He is rightly recognized as one of the foremost scholars in Wales.

I
WHAT IS SATANISM?

Satanism has been defined as a philosophy, a set of theological beliefs, or, in the broadest sense, an ideology. These Satanist beliefs are accompanied by signs and symbols, many of which are thought by some adherents to possess strange, innate powers. The broad spectrum of Satanism contains many different traditions and a number of them are very ancient.

One significant feature of Satanism is that the central figure – sometimes called the devil, sometimes called Lucifer – is generally admired and venerated by his followers.

This central entity, however, is regarded by some Satanists as a mere personification of their desire for power, or pleasure – or even as a personification of their ideology as a whole – rather than as a genuine *being* in his own right.

There are what may be termed religious Satanists, whose belief systems are based on Islamic, Judean, or Christian traditions. They go along with the broad idea that Satan, or Lucifer, was once an angel who rebelled against God (Yahweh/Jehovah) and led a group of other rebellious angels against the Deity and the loyal angels.

Originally, according to the book of Job, *the* Satan was a rank or function, rather than the name of an individual. His job was to be an *adversary*, an *accuser*, or a *prosecutor* in some sort of moral and ethical celestial court. From being the holder of a rank, or official position, in the cosmic judiciary, *the* Satan had become simply Satan – an individual with a name – by the time the New Testament Gospels were compiled. It is in this *personal* capacity that Satan becomes the tempter of Jesus.

Eschatology – the theology of the "Last Days" – regards Satan as the leader of the enemies of God and humanity, who will finally be destroyed at the end of the world.

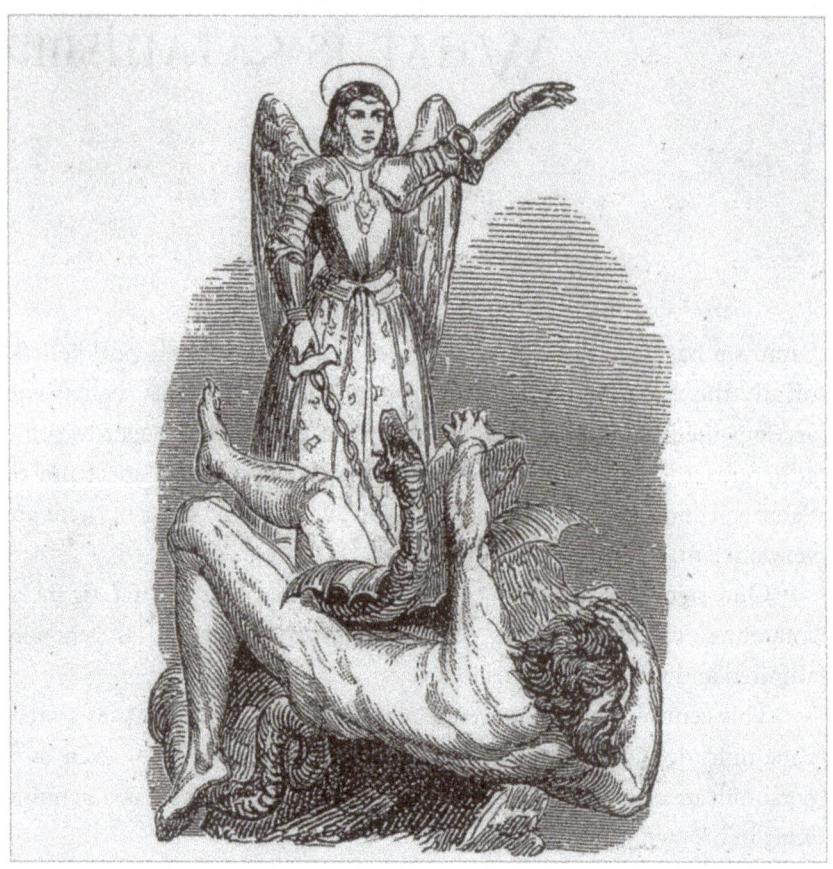

The archangel Michael destroys Satan at the End of the World.

The Battle of Armageddon is seen in these eschatological writings as the final conflict in the ultimate war between good and evil. The word *armageddon* translates as "hill of Megiddo." Megiddo was an ancient Middle Eastern city, located in present-day Israel, a few kilometres west of the Sea of Galilee (known to the ancient Romans as the Sea of Tiberius); various decisive historical battles were fought in the vicinity of Megiddo.

After Satan's final defeat at Armageddon — according to the book of Revelation — he and his followers will be thrown into Gehenna (a lake of sulphur that burns forever).

Later thinkers tended to regard Satan as some sort of allegory — especially after the publication of John Milton's *Paradise Lost* in 1667.

These ideas of Satan, and of his role in the fall of Adam and Eve as described in the Genesis account, are sometimes thought of as signifying a loss of faith or the striving of an individual to exert his will and personality against the will of God — as that divine will is represented by conventional and traditional religious teachings.

Some modern academic liberal theologians, however, would suggest that a truly loving God seeks to develop and enrich human individuality, encouraging us to be ourselves, rather than seeking to impose his will on us and subsuming his creation into himself. Although some Satanists may try to claim human individuality and independence as part of their belief system, many modern Christians would see their individuality and personal freedom as one of God's most precious gifts.

A further stage in the development of thought about the nature of Satan is to see him as a heroic character, and this aspect of him appeals to some groups of Satanists. In their minds, Satan becomes something approaching a romantic rebel leader. George Bernard Shaw's eighth play, *The Devil's Disciple*, has the hero, Dick Dudgeon, proclaiming himself to be the devil's disciple because of what he rightly regards as the cold hardness and cruelty of the worst forms of Christian Puritanism.

It was widely believed throughout the Middle Ages — and for a surprisingly long time afterward — that witchcraft and black magic relied upon Satan and his supporting demons for their power. An anti-witchcraft act was on the British statute books until as recently as 1951, when it was officially repealed.

Three years before that act was repealed in the United Kingdom, Herbert Arthur Sloane founded the Coven of Our Lady of Endor, named after the Witch of Endor, whose story is found in the first book of Samuel (chapter 28, verses 3–5). In it, King Saul had attacked all witches, wizards, and magicians and had cleared them out of his kingdom. However, in disguise, he then contacted the Witch of Endor and asked her to raise the spirit of the dead prophet Samuel so that Saul could ask the seer's advice. Samuel's spirit reprimands the king and tells him that he and his sons will be killed in battle next day — this duly coming to pass. Some Christian sects who are vehemently opposed to all forms of contact with the next world suggest that it was not the spirit of Samuel but Satan who spoke to Saul.

The serpent of Eden worshipped by the Ophites.

The Endor Coven is also known as Ophite Cultus Satanas or Sathanas. Their religious views are largely Gnostic and the serpent in their interpretation of the Garden of Eden story is referred to as Ophite because a few Gnostic sects operating in Syria and Egypt toward the end of the first century were known variously as Ophites, Serpentinians, and Ophians, and were reputed to worship serpents.

Sloane was inspired to found his organization because of what he reported as a childhood meeting in the woods with a horned being that he later thought was Satan.

As distinct from Sloane's group, dating from 1948, the Church of Satan was founded on Walpurgisnacht, April 30, 1966. Its then leader,

Anton LaVey, ran a group known as the Order of the Trapezoid in San Francisco, California. LaVey remained as its High Priest until his death in 1997. Part of the ritual and liturgy of the Church of Satan included Satanist weddings and funerals. LaVey also appeared in a number of films, including *The Devil's Rain* starring Ernest Borgnine and William Shatner.

There seems to be an ironic paradox in the name Church of Satan because one of its prominent leaders, Peter H. Gilmore, has allegedly summed up its central belief by saying: "Satanism begins with atheism. We begin with the universe and say, 'It's indifferent. There's no God. There's no devil. No one cares!'"

LaVey had pronounced ideas about the importance of achievement and accomplishment. Success in a wide variety of fields was important to him. In the mid-1970s he set about removing people from his Church of Satan if they hadn't accomplished anything notable in some other field. He didn't want Church of Satan members to use their rank in his church as a substitute for success in other areas. Wealth and fame became the criteria for promotion in the Church of Satan. Could this, perhaps, be regarded as a double-edged sword? By promoting only those with claims to worldly wealth and fame, was the inference that membership of the Church of Satan led to wealth and fame – rather than vice-versa?

The so-called "Satanic Panic" of the 1980s centred on media hints that there were criminal activities going on in a big way in the Church of Satan. LaVey, Gilmore, Rice, Parfrey, Nadramia, and other prominent leaders made many media appearances to refute these allegations, and were subsequently justified by an FBI report that demonstrated the inaccuracy and invalidity of the criminal accusations being made against their church. They then concentrated on making documentary films, producing magazines, including *The Black Flame*, and Boyd Rice's music – all with Satanist themes.

When LaVey died in 1997, he was replaced as leader by Blanche Barton, who was in turn replaced by Peter Gilmore and Peggy Nadramia, who are currently in charge of the church.

Satanism gained official recognition in the armed services in 2004 when a technician serving on a British ship was officially recognized as a registered Satanist.

The apparent paradox of regarding Satan as a model or mode of behaviour, rather than as a supernatural entity, underlies the belief system expressed by the Church of Satan. Gilmore is on record as suggesting that belief in paranormal or supernatural entities is an abdication of human reason. He takes the old Hebrew idea of the Satan as an adversary or "opposer" a stage further and regards the Satan simply as the attitude of anyone who asks questions or expresses rational curiosity. Following Gilmore's thinking in that direction would seem to include a great many rational and objective scientists within his definition of Satanism!

From another perspective, Satanism may be thought of as a belief system that incorporates a number of attitudes. It recommends indulgence of the senses and appetites as opposed to abstinence. It advocates living for the moment and experiencing everything that can be enjoyed in the here and the now, rather than dreaming of things in the future that may never be attainable.

Satanists claim that they are interested in what they define as "real wisdom" as distinct from illusions, delusions, and the shallow comfort of self-deceit. Another principle is summed up as taking revenge on those who have wronged us — yet, at the same time giving help and kindness to those who are genuinely grateful for it. Kindness offered to those who don't appreciate it or return it is a waste of time in the Satanist calendar. This attitude also applies to the concept of responsibility in the Satanist code. If we encounter people who show responsibility in their dealings with us, it is acceptable to show responsibility and integrity in our dealings with them.

Humanity's place in the scale of life is simply as another animal among animals — nothing better, and, perhaps, worse than many in terms of human viciousness and brutality.

When Satanism is compared and contrasted with those religious systems that recognize certain behaviours as "sinful," it tends to favour those forbidden behaviours on the grounds that they lead to satisfaction and gratification. Stealing, for example, to a Satanist is a quick and easy way of acquiring wealth and property. Adultery is a quick and easy way to sexual gratification. Murdering a dangerous enemy before he can murder you is a quick and easy way to reduce risk or remove a troublesome rival.

Just as Satanism advocates living by committing what the great world religions refer to as "sins," so it has its own list of "sins" — behaviours that are regarded by Satanists as being anti-satanic. The first of these is stupid or foolish behaviour; acting irrationally works against satisfaction and gratification. Pretentiousness and self-deceit of any kind are also regarded as follies that Satanists are recommended to avoid. Satanists see themselves as realistic, factual, and pragmatic. To pretend is to deceive yourself; again, it can be said to hinder satisfaction and gratification. Solipsism also falls under the Satanists' hammer. Not the easiest of philosophical concepts to define, solipsism can be explained as the basic belief that there is no reality outside the mind of the thinker. Solipsists would argue that the self is all that we can say with absolute certainty exists. Another way of putting it is that solipsism argues that the idea of the existence of anything outside the thinker's own mind cannot be justified. Everything in the external environment might not be there at all. A solipsist might well regard her belief system as an extreme form of scepticism tantamount to saying: "Nothing except my mind — and what it creates — really exists!" Satanists include solipsism in their list of sins.

Collectivism, going with the group, following the herd, being a conformist is regarded as a sin against Satanism. To be a well-behaved traditionalist gets in the way of that individualistic search for gratification and satisfaction that is at the core of Satanism. Another of the Satanist sins is a lack of perspective. To be successful in the endless satanic quest for gratification and satisfaction, the Satanist has to look at life from every angle — he has to be the fox as well as the hound before deciding what to do to obtain maximum satisfaction! Only when the Satanist has looked at all the possible outcomes from all the points of view of which he is aware, can satisfaction and gratification be optimized by appropriate action.

Then there is the question — taking perspectives a stage further — of the historical perspective. The Satanist is expected to remember orthodox ideologies that controlled societies in the past: Greek philosophy, Roman militarism and imperialism, Babylonian commerce, Indian mysticism, and the Chinese veneration of wisdom. By comparing and contrasting his quest for personal satisfaction and gratification with those historical perspectives, the Satanist expects to facilitate the pursuit of pleasure. There is also a warning in the list of satanic sins against the wrong sort of pride. In the Satanist code, pride can be counterproductive. It can get in the way of the achievement of satisfaction if it is unjustified. The great world heavyweight boxing champion John L. Sullivan (1858-1918), known as the Boston Strong Boy, would announce as he entered the ring: "I'm John L. Sullivan and I can lick any man alive!" And it was true — he could! His was completely justifiable pride. It is the pride that falls into the same category as self-deception which Satanists regard as one of the "sins" that get in the way of the personal success, satisfaction, and gratification that they regard as their ultimate objectives.

Other aspects of Satanism include various lifestyles and methods of living. Satanists decline from giving advice — unless they are specifically asked. They do not share their troubles with others. They believe that if they have used magical powers successfully, they must acknowledge the reality of those powers — denying them is to lose them.

A strange marriage between some forms of modern Satanist thinking and technology has been referred to as the desirability of creating androids to become artificial humanoid companions — or slaves — to dominant Satanists. Such creations are frequently the subject of science fiction and science fantasy narratives, where the plots involve their dawning awareness of who and what they really are, and their attempts to rebel and escape.

Certain semi-secret groups of Satanists are referred to as "grottoes." When formed, the members meet socially, and in some instances perform magic together.

Another organization that needs to be included in any general understanding of Satanism is the group known as the Temple of Set, which was established in the 1970s by Michael Aquino. Like the Church of Satan, and much that is included in general Satanism, it venerates the individual and aims at what it refers to as "enlightenment." This seems to refer to the finding of ways to facilitate personal satisfaction and gratification. The organization takes its name from the Egyptian god Set, or Seth, and its principles are referred to as Setianism.

This opening chapter has attempted to provide broad answers to the question of what Satanism really is — and two clear fields have emerged from the survey. The first may be termed religious Satanism and expresses a belief in the devil, Satan, or Lucifer as a person, a supernatural entity, worshipped by his followers in the way that the classical Greco-Roman gods and the Norse gods were worshipped by their followers. Their deity responds to their worship by rewarding them with worldly success, pleasure, gratification, and magical powers. The second type of Satanism is atheistic. Neither gods nor demons have any real existence. This type of Satanism is merely attitudinal or philosophical — a way of achieving worldly success and gratification through thinking, speaking, and acting in accordance with what are defined as satanic principles. The self is venerated instead of any external entity with paranormal powers.

2
THE EARLY HISTORY OF SATANISM

Strange pictures of half-human, half-animal entities have been discovered in cave paintings in the Dordogne region of France. These have been interpreted in different ways by archaeologists. Some regard them as evidence of early Shamanism, while others consider that the half-human, half-beast form indicates belief in an evil supernatural entity — along the lines of the much later Minotaur of Knossos.

A number of archaeologists suggest that there is reasonable evidence for the appearance of some types of primitive, quasi-religious behaviour as early as the dawn of Palaeolithic times, more than three hundred thousand years ago. Evidence of ancient burial rites in the area provide vital insight into the religious thoughts of those who carried them out; and the dating of what may be regarded as the earliest religious behaviour seems to coincide with the emergence of *Homo neanderthalensis* and *Homo sapiens*. This earliest quasi-religious behaviour is analyzed by some theologians, sociologists, and archaeologists as containing elements of animism, magic, ritual, and myth. It is also widely

Half-human, half-animal entity from the caves at Dordogne in France.

thought that what might be termed ethical and moral behavioural constraints as components of religious thinking did not enter the equation until several more millennia had passed.

Well over sixty thousand years ago, Neanderthals seem to have had ideas about life after death, and grave goods were buried with the dead for them to use in the next world. Evidence from Shanidar, in Iraq, is significant. American archaeologist Ralph Stefan Solecki, of Columbia University, investigated the Shanidar Cave in the Zagros Mountains of Kurdistan from 1957 to 1961, and found nine Neanderthal skeletons along with evidence of ritual burial customs. Stone tools and animal bones were also found there.

At a limestone cave known as the Kebara Cave, on the western side of the Carmel Range, Professor Ofer Bar-Yosef found human remains dating

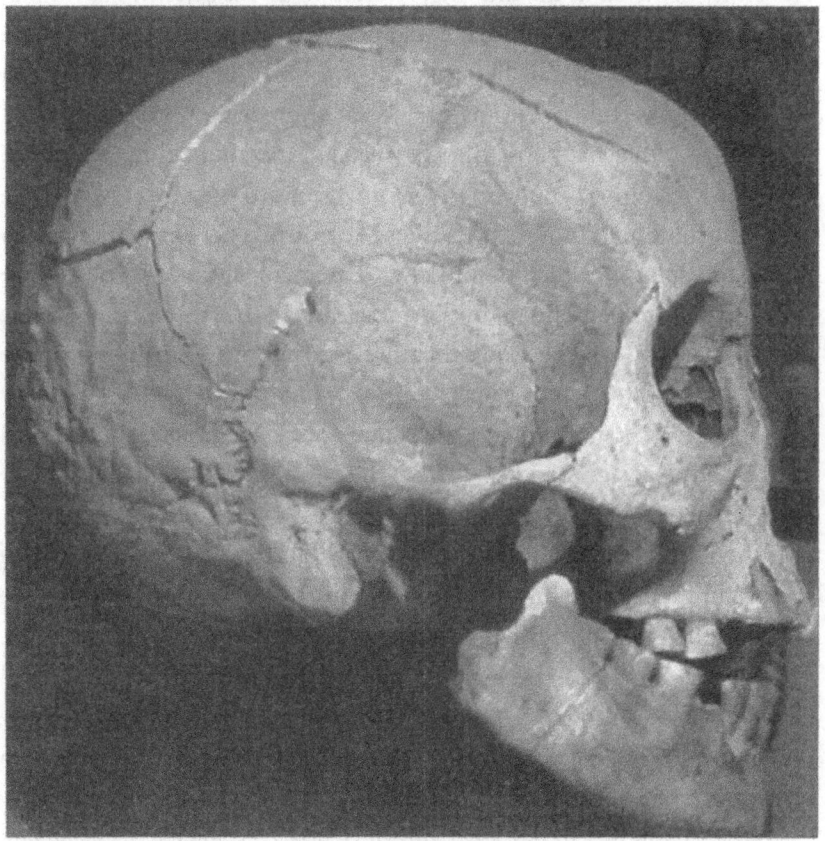

Ancient human skull.

back some fifty thousand years. This site also indicated religious burial rituals similar to those seen at Shanidar.

What is often referred to by archaeologists as the most spectacular Neanderthal finding of all time was discovered in a place called the Krapina Cave, located in Hrvatsko Zagoje in Croatia. Close to one thousand bones, believed to belong to about eighty separate individuals — almost all of them being young adults aged between fifteen and twenty-five — have been uncovered there.

In the Ariège Department of France, in the Montesquieu-Avantès, is the Cave of the Three Brothers, referred to as *Trois Frères* because it was discovered in 1910 by the three sons of Count Bégouen. In this cave was found a remarkable piece of artwork, approximately twenty thousand years old, which has never been satisfactorily interpreted or explained. The entity depicted in the drawing, referred to as *The Sorcerer*, has human feet and muscular hind legs that could be either human or animal. There is a prominent bushy tail like the tail of a horse or a greatly enlarged squirrel, a powerful, full-stomached body with disproportionally small forelimbs — rather like those of a *Tyrannosaurus rex*. Something similar to a cartoon version of a human face is turned toward the observer, and the skull is surmounted by a pair of antler-like horns. There are ears on each side of the cranium which point skyward at an angle from the head. The entity appears to be bearded, but it is unclear whether this was simply the natural markings on the stone that give this impression or if it was the Stone-Age artist's attempt to give his creation a beard. The whole thing has a classically demonic appearance, and could well have been intended to represent a personified force of evil. If so, it may be one more example of the ancient roots of Satanism.

The four Tsodilo Hills in the Western Kalahari in Botswana are the site of hundreds of prehistoric carvings and paintings. One aspect of the Tsodilo Hills links it to the Gnostic sects referred to in the first chapter. They operated in Syria and Egypt toward the end of the first century and were known variously as Ophites, Serpentinians, and Ophians because they were reputed to worship serpents. A large stone in the form of a serpent can be seen in the Tsodilo Hills.

When Laurens van der Post, author of *The Lost World of the Kalahari*, visited the site, he encountered one inexplicable problem after another:

Entity from the Cave of Trois Frères.

tape recorders failed to record, cameras jammed, and swarms of bees attacked his expedition. He later found that two of his employees had broken the local Tsodilo religious laws by killing animals in the vicinity of the decorated hills. Van der Post wrote an apology to the local spirit-gods and buried it in the earth below some very striking ancient rock paintings. It is alleged that this cured the problems – the spirit-gods of Tsodilo were believed to have forgiven the transgressors after the apology was made!

The San people, who have lived in the area for many thousands of years, believe that their gods – not all of whom are benign – live inside

The enormous figure of the Cerne Abbas Giant outlined on a Dorset hillside. He bears a striking resemblance to the stylized males depicted on the Tsodilo Hills.

the caverns in the Tsodilo Hills. The depictions of stylized male figures among the Tsodilo artwork show them in a state of sexual arousal like the famous Cerne Abbas Giant of Dorset, England.

Emile Bächler, an expert in the field of archaeology, suggests that there is evidence found at number of ancient, inhabited caves that indicate that the Neanderthals practised both totemism and animal worship – namely bear worship. Also known as Arctolatry, bear worship was most commonly practised in the circumpolar regions and was prevalent in Finland before the arrival of Christianity. It still survives in the cultures of the Ainu, Nivkhs, and Sami peoples.

One aspect of the bear cult was the belief that the creatures were involved in the ladder of human reincarnation. After the annual festival was celebrated in January and February, a bear was killed and eaten so that it could return to a happy state with the gods and departed tribal spirits, ready for further incarnations. In some accounts of the ritual, the bear's skull was placed on top of a sacred old pine tree known as the *kallohonka*. This was thought to place the bear's soul nearer to the sky and facilitate its return to the abode of the spirits.

Although normally seen as a benign figure, closely involved with human welfare, there may have been occasions when followers believed that the bear-spirit became angry with them for some real or imagined failure. In those instances it is said that the bear would become a demonic creature — the adversary, enemy, and judge of the people, whom it might then decide to punish.

There also seems to have been a link between animal worship and primitive hunting magic in Palaeolithic times. One ceremony appears to have involved killing a bear and burying the skull and body separately, but near to a clay statue of a bear that had been draped in real bear fur.

The Inuit peoples of the Arctic believe in a variety of demons and evil spirits. Their belief systems are very ancient, and may throw some light on the earliest roots of Satanism. They believe in an evil spirit called Aipalookvik who lives in the sea and attacks boats and boatmen. Another evil entity that resembles a hairless dog is known as Keelut.

The earliest of the Iroquois myths and legends has certain parallels with both the Greek story of Persephone and Hades and with the Roman tale of Pluto and Proserpina. In all three cases (Iroquois, Greek, and Roman), the beautiful daughter of the Earth Mother is abducted by the god of the underworld but later rescued. The Iroquois Earth Mother, Eithinoha, lost her daughter Onatha, the Spirit of Wheat, when the girl was abducted by the Spirit of Evil. Onatha was imprisoned below ground in his dark kingdom until she was rescued by the vastly powerful sun god. Although the basis of all three myths is explanatory and sets out to give reasons for the existence of the seasons, each also contains trace elements of the sources of evil. Though Hades and Pluto are not unredeemably evil, the entity referred to as the Evil Spirit in the Iroquois myth certainly is.

Another early strand of Satanism may be associated with the ancient Greek traditions centring on the faun-like Pan.

Although some aspects of Pan are benign — he is associated with shepherds, the mountains, wild and natural scenery, hunting, and music — there are other perspectives which are more sinister. He is depicted as satyr-like in appearance, with the horns and legs of a goat and the associated insatiable sexual desire. As a fertility god, his pursuit of nymphs — and human girls — is at the core of many of the Pan legends.

Pan is also associated with Arcadia, a place regarded by some theologians and folklorists as almost the equivalent of Eden: a rural paradise. This reference to Arcadia relates to the sinister mysteries of Rennes-le-Château in the south of France, where the mysterious priest, Bérenger Saunière, became unaccountably wealthy at the close of the nineteenth century. Part of that mystery involves the enigmatic painter Nicolas Poussin (1594-1665), whose most famous canvas was *The Shepherds of Arcadia*. This painting shows three shepherds and a nubile young shepherdess (of the kind who would have appealed to Pan) examining a tomb on which is inscribed the words *Et in Arcadia ego*.

It has been open to several translation attempts ranging through the idea that the dead man in the tomb has gone on to the paradise of Arcadia; that even in the perfect rural idyll of Arcadia, Death is present; or that the speaker is Pan himself, saying that he is to be found in Arcadia.

Associating Pan with the mysterious tomb in Poussin's painting brings up the strange legend encapsulated in the phrase "Great Pan is dead!" This strange confusion over the "death" of an immortal god originated with the Greek historian Plutarch (A.D. 46-120), who wrote that during the reign of the Roman Emperor Tiberius, a sailor named Thamus heard a voice calling to him across the waves, instructing him to announce the death of Pan to all and sundry when he reached Palodes, then a small port on the eastern side of the Bosphorus, the narrow straits separating Europe from Asia.

What could this so-called "death" of Pan really mean? Was it intended to indicate a passing of the old, natural order, which the god Pan personified? Certainly the worship of Pan — even in the twenty-first century — is far from dead. Modern pagans and worshippers of Nature have the highest regard for him — and he is still venerated in many of their rituals and ceremonies. Is it his powerful sexuality that has made him into a semi-demonic figure — especially in the eyes of puritans and religious celibates? His horns and goat hindquarters and legs have certainly associated him with traditional images of Satan and Lucifer.

Another fertility deity that has attracted the opprobrium of many religious writers for millennia is Baal. The word *baal* simply translates as "lord" or "master" — a title rather than a name. There was an avoidance of using the proper name of a god such as Hadad, ruler of fertility, rain, and thunder, unless you were one of his duly appointed priests, and so he would generally be referred to as Baal instead. The title Baal was also used for any number of local gods, who were generally referred to as false gods by the writers of the Hebrew scriptures. They were frequently accompanied by female consorts, the Astarte/Ashtoreth.

These female consorts were worshipped as both warriors by day and love goddesses by night. They were depicted in their warrior role as carrying bows and looking like amazons, and in their love and fertility role as beautiful naked women rather like Venus or Aphrodite. The sexual rites that were part of their worship distanced them from their Israelite critics, and religious prostitution was practised by temple prostitutes following the worship of Astarte.

It may be reasonable to assume that the opposition to both Baal worship and the sexual ceremonies that accompanied the worship of Astarte, led to an association of Baal and Astarte with Satanism, black magic, and demonology.

Another very ancient demonic female entity is encapsulated in the legends of Lilith. According to very ancient myths, she was created from the soil, the dust of the Earth — the *adamah* — in the same way as Adam. The legends are confused as to whether she was married to the archangel Samael first, and then enticed away from him to marry Adam — or whether she was Adam's first wife, but quarrelled with him and left him to marry Samael. In either case, she is listed in legend as the wife of both. Samael is also rendered as Sammael and Sadil. Talmudic lore is ambiguous about him: he is the angel of death, and is regarded as both good *and* evil. In another version of the legends surrounding Lilith, Samael is said to have disguised himself as the serpent, tempted Eve, and then seduced her — the evil in him leading to the birth of Cain, the first murderer.

The legendary Lilith has exceptionally long and beautiful hair, and wings that enable her to fly. In the version of the legend in which she was married to Samael *before* her union with Adam, she was a wildly passionate and independent entity, whose partnership with Adam led to the birth of numerous demons, known as Shedim, who are responsible for diseases, accidents, injuries, and most of the difficulties which confront humanity. Just as Lilith's wild, rebellious spirit had driven her away from Samael, so, according to this version of the legend, it brought her into conflict with Adam, who tried unsuccessfully to make her understand that he was the master in their partnership. She would have none of it, and left!

Adam appealed to God, who responded by sending three angels to fetch her back: Sammangelof, Sansenoi, and Senoi. They failed, and so God created Eve as a replacement for Lilith.

As the legend proceeds, Lilith becomes known as Meyalleleth, meaning "the howling night demon." Far from being a unique female demon, Lilith is opposed by two others, known as Makhlath the Dancer and her equally powerful and sinister daughter, Agrath the Beater.

Some pointers to the ancient origins of Satanism may be found in these legends — the various demonesses were regarded as the *mothers* of evil.

Just as the legendary Lilith and her rival demonesses are shrouded in myth and mystery, so is the cult of Mithras. Little is known of the way in which the mysteries were performed, or what they actually meant to their adherents. What little can be filtered out of the many underground temples dedicated to Mithras suggests that he was a benign god who defended his followers from the dangers that were launched at them by evil spirits and demons. The Greek root from which the modern word *mysteries* is derived originally meant "with closed lips and eyes" — and such were the mysteries that were associated with Mithraism.

Although it is generally argued that Mithraism did not get started much before 1400 B.C., there is evidence that it may have gone back much farther, having originated more or less simultaneously in both ancient Persia and the Indus Valley. Its value in any research into the primitive origins of Satanism lies in its unyielding opposition to all things evil: because Mithraism was seen as a bulwark against evil in all its forms, the existence of evil is implied. By teaching their followers that Mithras would defend them against devils, demons, and evil spirits, the priests of Mithras were expressing their firm belief that such defences were essential.

The basic belief system was that Mithras had been born from a rock, hence his inordinate strength and valour in combatting evil in all its forms. He is also associated with the slaughter of a magical bull, even though his goodness and kindness were so great that he was unwilling to slay it. There is something of a creation myth in the slaying of the noble bull, as from the different parts of its body came all the green plants: its spine turned into corn and its blood became vines from which rich red wine was produced. Initiates went through seven grades of membership:

the raven, the bridegroom, the soldier, the lion, the Persian, the messenger of the sun, and the father.

Buddhism also provides clues to the origins of Satanism, especially when the principles of Satanism as described in the first chapter are focused on the individual's desire for personal power and pleasure. Referring briefly to the life of Gautama, who was born to enjoy every luxury but who turned his back on all personal desires and went off to seek enlightenment, he was subjected to many temptations by Mara, the evil one. Mara sent his three beautiful, talented, and seductive daughters to tempt Gautama away from his quest for enlightenment, but irresistible as the three delicious young females would have been to anyone else, Gautama took no notice of all their efforts to seduce him.

Furious because of their failure, their demonic father rose into the air, mounted the clouds like steeds, and hurled his terrifying disk at Gautama. That weapon could slice through a Himalayan peak but had no effect at all on Gautama. Mara was defeated. Here again, as with Mithraism, the forces of evil are revealed by studying the attitude and responses of a good, noble spiritual leader. Once again, it is possible to study the nature of evil by studying what goodness does in order to fight evil and to triumph over it.

Some fundamental concepts underlying a dualistic theology as an explanation for the origins of evil, and, by association, the origins of Satanism, have been seen by some theorists as an indication that extraterrestrials were involved with our remote ancestors. Two or more rival groups of such entities, it is suggested, presented themselves to Palaeolithic humanity as the representatives of "good" and "evil" and cautioned our remote ancestors about involvement with their rivals. Religious explanations about "war in Heaven" would not be irreconcilable with these ideas of rival would-be colonizers. The development of such theories brings in the idea of genetic engineering and the "creation" of *Homo sapiens* — again, the idea of extraterrestrial technologists working on our ancestors is not irreconcilable with traditional religious versions of creation.

The earliest origins of Satanism may, therefore, be examined as a number of distinct possibilities: the version suggested by the Abrahamic religions involving Satan's fall from Heaven; the theories arising from ancient cave art depicting strange quasi-human entities as they existed in Palaeolithic imagination; or the work of technically advanced extraterrestrial colonists.

Satanism in the Middle East

One of the oldest Stone-Age settlements in the Middle East was Nevali Cori, which was excavated and explored in 1993 by Professor Harald Hauptmann and his team from the University of Heidelberg. The construction of the Ataturk Dam meant that the waters of the River Euphrates inundated the site.

Many flint tools were discovered there, and the houses were of a remarkably advanced pattern for a settlement more than ten thousand years old. A number of these houses also contained skulls and incomplete human skeletons.

The many carvings discovered there included larger-than-life-sized human heads with hair resembling serpents, as well as birds, human hands, and humanoid statues cut from the local limestone. Fired clay miniature depictions of human beings were also found. This suggests that the inhabitants had mastered elementary pre-pottery-making techniques.

Soon after its discovery in 1958, another ancient site at Catal Hoyuk was explored by James Mellaart in the early 1960s. Further work was done years later by a Cambridge University team led by Ian Hodder in 1993. Excavations provided figurines that seemed to represent either a demoness or the Earth Mother goddess. Male gods or demons were also represented among the many figurines found. Were they simply meant to be Baal and Ashtoreth, or were they something more sinister?

A number of the archaeologists working on the site at Catal Hoyuk were of the opinion that many of the skeletons that were found with separated skulls were buried in that way as a sign of respect, or an awareness of their special prominence in that Palaeolithic society. Could there be other interpretations? If the soul or spirit was believed by these ancient peoples to reside in the skull, were these skulls then separated to prevent the return of the people so treated? If the idea was, in fact, to prevent their return to the land of the living, was it because they had been singularly dangerous and evil during their earthly lives? Was it feared that death had transformed them into demons and demonesses?

In one of the most ancient Persian religions — originating at or before the time of Catal Hoyuk — Ahriman, also known as Arimanius and Angra Mainya, was the god of evil, equivalent to Satan, the devil, or Lucifer. The god of goodness was Ahura Mazda, also known as Ohrmazd or Oromasdes (the spellings of both ancient names vary considerably). This religion was classically dualistic: equally balanced forces of good and evil opposed each other.

According to the ancient teachings of Zoroaster, also known as Zarathustra, there were powerful, divine entities known as Ahuras. Their leader, the great and powerful Ahura Mazda, opted to be the force of goodness. His followers, the Ahuras, also chose goodness. His opponent, Ahriman, leader of the Daevas, chose to be evil — and the Daevas followed him along this path. Zoroastrianism also taught that all beings have free will and must choose to be evil or good.

Unlike the ideas of God and Satan in the Abrahamic religions, Ohrmazd and Ahriman were limited as to what they could do. Ohrmazd was unlimited by time but had certain spatial limitations. He was not seen as omnipresent like the omnipotent God of the Abrahamic religions. Ahriman was even more limited — both time and space presented barriers for him. Time was his particular limitation, as he knew that at the end of time he would be defeated by Ohrmazd.

In the beginning, Ohrmazd was aware of Ahriman — but Ahriman was not aware of him. Eventually, however, Ahriman learned of his good opponent, and that the battle would eventually end with Ohrmazd's victory. So great was the goodness and tolerance of Ohrmazd that he offered to end the war if Ahriman would change his ways and accept goodness — this, tragically, he refused to do, and the war continues until the end of time, when Ahriman will face inevitable destruction.

According to a different tradition, Zeranism, Ohrmazd, and Ahriman are actually brothers: the sons of Zurvan the All and his wife — who is actually his own female self. As the brothers were thought of as equal, so the dualist theology arose.

Ahriman, according to this tradition, created all the evil in the universe to counteract all the good that Ohrmazd created. Ahriman was responsible for every kind of sinful behaviour and all the natural disasters, as well: locusts, ants, lack of faith, diseases of all types, pride, witchcraft and evil magic, cannibalism, and deformity.

Ahriman's evil work also included various attempts to kill or tempt away from goodness Zarathustra, the prophet. A demon named Buiti was sent first, but failed miserably. Ahriman then had a go at it himself – and also failed dismally.

Each of the leaders of good and evil is accompanied by seven powerful followers. In Ohrmazd's case these are archangels, or Amesha Spenta. Ahriman's principal followers are archdemons. Their names are sometimes given as (spellings vary): Aeshma, Aka Manah, Indra, Naonhaithva, Sauru, Taurvi, and Zairitsha.

According to the sacred writings in the Farvardin Yasht, there will be a number of saviours referred to as Saoshyants. The third and greatest of these Saoshyants will be the son of Zarathustra and a virgin mother. His followers will be ideal human beings who will destroy demons and bring in a reign of righteousness. His work will lead to the resurrection of the dead to eternal happiness, and evil will vanish forever.

Another ancient Middle Eastern legend concerning the inculcation of evil refers to a strange entity called Zohak. His father was a desert king, and Zohak was cursed with more ambition than is good for a man. Ahriman worked on the self-centred and greedy Zohak until he had become a tool of evil. Under Ahriman's influence, Zohak murdered his father and took the throne. The next stage of Ahriman's plans was to ingratiate himself into Zohak's palace in the role of cook. The people were naturally vegetarian, until the new cook taught them to eat meat. Zohak enjoyed the new meat menus so much that he planned to express his pleasure by rewarding the demon-cook. Ahriman requested permission to kiss King Zohak's shoulders as his reward. Once this had been accomplished, Ahriman vanished from the palace. Where Ahriman had kissed the unfortunate desert monarch, a hideous black snake sprang from each of Zohak's shoulders. They grew again each time the royal surgeon hacked them off! Nothing seemed able to prevent this recurrence. Ahriman reappeared, pretending to be a famous doctor/magician, and told Zohak that the snakes needed to be fed regularly on human brains — nice and warm and fresh from the skull! These instructions were duly followed. The result was that Zohak was transformed from a human being into a singularly unpleasant demon, one of Ahriman's staunchest and most dangerous supporters.

The story of Zohak continues by introducing the originally good Jemshid, who had succumbed to the sin of pride as the result of Ahriman's temptations. Jemshid came into conflict with Zohak, who defeated him and gave orders to saw him in half.

Zohak then reigned for a millennium, during which time unspeakable evil flourished. It was finally prophesied in a dream that he would be destroyed by a heroic young prince. Rather like the evil King Herod at the time of the birth of Jesus, Zohak arranged for the murder of all baby boys. Despite all Zohak's fiendishly brutal precautions, however, Feridun — the prince who was destined to destroy him — was taken beyond his reach by his prudent mother, and eventually grew up to throw down Zohak. Feridun then established a long reign of peace and goodness.

The Phoenician god Melqart may also have played a significant part in the early development of proto-Satanism in the Middle East. Also rendered as Melkart and Melkarth, his name meant "Lord of the City" or "King of the City." In that capacity, he protected Tyre. His counterpart, Eshmun, protected Sidon. In Tyre, the High Priest of Melqart ranked immediately below the king.

Melqart appears to have been the deified development of an actual early historical King of Tyre, perhaps the founder of the dynasty. Confusingly, owing to the later widespread Greek influence, Melqart became indentified with Hercules (Herakles), and became known accordingly as the Hercules of Tyre, or the Tyrian Hercules. Because of this later identification with the benign and heroic Hellenistic demi-god Hercules, some of Melqart's proto-satanistic aspects were camouflaged.

Melqart's fame spread far beyond Tyre and he was apparently worshipped as far away as Spain. His name appears on an inscription on a basalt stela, or pillar, dating from 1000 B.C., which was excavated in Bredsh near Aleppo in Syria just before the outbreak of the Second World War. The stela was created on the orders of King Bar Hadad III, also known as Ben Hadad of Damascus, who came to the throne after the death of his father, Hazael. There are biblical references to him in II Kings, 13. The association of Melqart with Satanism, and opposition to the Hebrew God Yahweh, can almost certainly be traced to the dramatic conflict of the prophet Elijah with the prophets of Baal — almost certainly the prophets serving Melqart.

In the first book of Kings, Chapter 18, Elijah tells the evil King Ahab, husband of the even more evil Queen Jezebel, to summon the prophets of Baal (almost certainly Melqart) for a contest on Mount Carmel. A vast crowd assembles to watch the proceedings. Each side is to prepare a sacrifice and then to call on their respective gods, Baal and Yahweh, to light the sacrifice miraculously. The god who lights the sacrifice will be acknowledged to be the only true God and will be worshipped accordingly. The contest duly takes place and Elijah's sacrifice is lit. The prophets of Baal and Ashtoreth are massacred.

In addition to these biblical references, the ancient Greek historian Herodotus (484-425 B.C.) has a valuable contribution to make to the knowledge of Melqart. He travelled extensively and consulted many witnesses. Although some of his accounts are questionable in the light of modern scholarship, many of them shed useful light on the history that he investigated. He actually visited Tyre as part of his research and wrote that there was a temple there dedicated to Hercules. Herodotus says that it was greatly venerated at the time of his visit, when it was filled with offerings, and he was particularly impressed by two beautiful pillars, one made of gold and the other encrusted with *smaragdos*, which translates from the Greek as "emerald.' These two pillars impressed Herodotus most because of the way that they shone in the darkness. When he asked about the age of the temple, the priests told him that it had been built well over 2,300 years before his visit — taking it back to approximately 2800 B.C.

Another famous ancient historian, Josephus, who lived and worked during the first century A.D., maintained that Hiram I, King of Tyre from 965-935 B.C., had rebuilt the ancient Temples of Melqart (Hercules) and Ashtart and re-roofed them with cedar from Lebanon.

As the Phoenician worshippers of Melqart spread ever westward and established their colonies, the name of Melqart was invoked for legal and business reasons when contracts were sworn. Temples or shrines were then built to Melqart as the protector of the traders. In the Sicilian

Phoenician colonies in the fourth century B.C., Melqart's head appeared on the coinage.

Moloch, another ancient Middle Eastern deity who may well have had a profound influence on the origins of Satanism, can be rendered as Molech, Molekh, Molek, or Moloc. The root consonants of his name — m, l, and k — can represent the idea of kingship, or they can be understood as a particular type of sacrifice — animal or human — in which the victim is burned alive. Moloch was known throughout the Middle East and in Africa, as well. Ammonites, Hebrews, Phoenicians, and Canaanites all had records of him in one form or another. Leviticus 18, verse 21, gives very strict and unequivocal instructions to the Hebrews that none of their children are to be passed through the fire to Moloch. Later commentaries on Moloch, and the fire ceremony, suggest that the effigy of Moloch was made of brass and that the hands of the idol were outstretched to receive the victim, whose cries of agony were drowned by the priests beating their drums. Other detailed information records that the Moloch idol was hollow and divided into seven separate compartments. Flour was placed in one compartment, doves in another; a ewe and a ram occupied two more; a calf and an ox occupied the fifth and sixth chambers; and a human child was placed in the last compartment.

The fire below the statue was ignited and all of the contents were burned. During and after the Punic Wars between Rome and Carthage, several Roman accounts mentioned the cruelty of the Carthaginians, claiming that they had sacrificed children to their evil god Moloch, whom they also referred to as Kronos.

John Milton's *Paradise Lost* describes Moloch as one of Satan's most dangerous and evil lieutenants:

> First Moloch, horrid King besmear'd with blood
> Of human sacrifice, and parents' tears,
> Though, for the noyse of Drums and Timbrels loud,
> Their children's cries unheard that passed through fire
> To his grim Idol.

Another very sinister and evil Persian demon was known as Apaosa/Apaosha, who brought excessive heat, the accompanying drought, and the

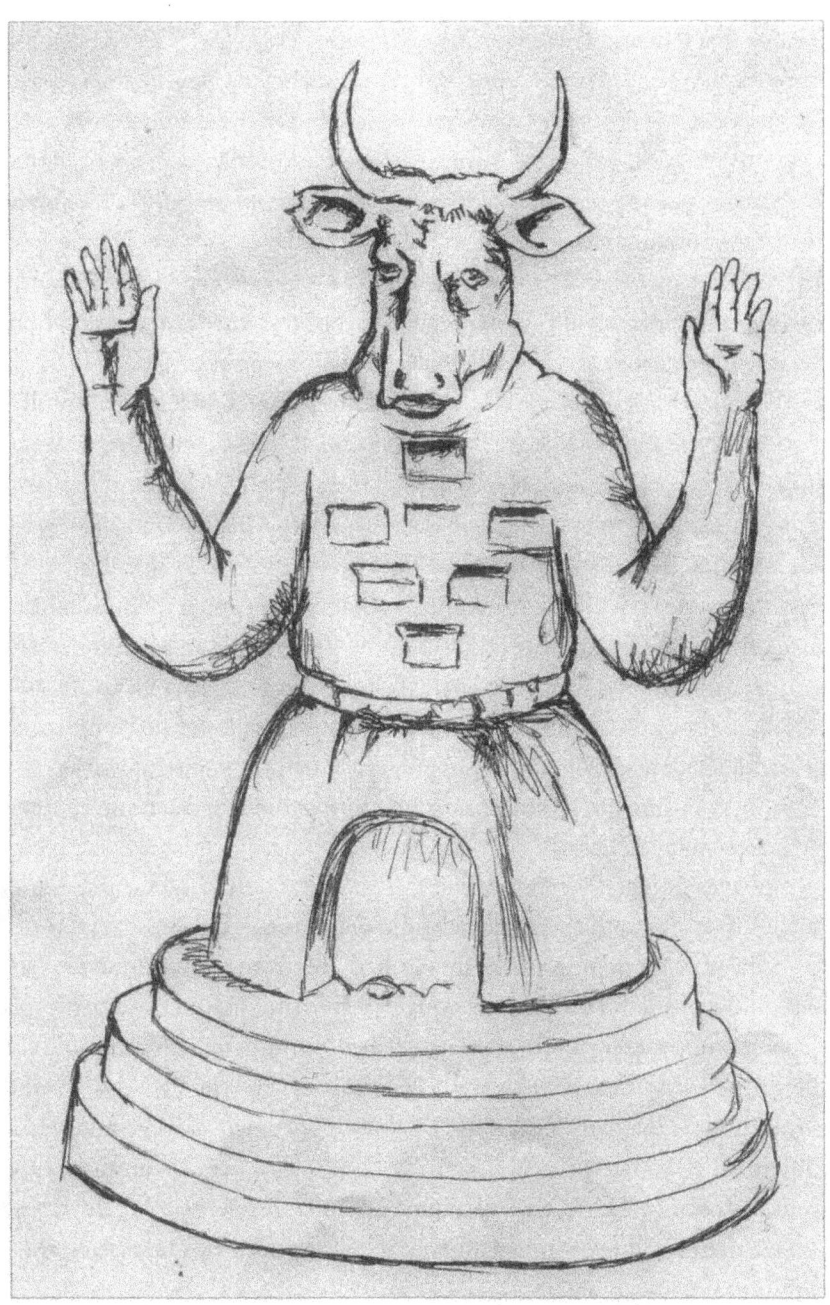

Moloch

famine that followed it. He was opposed by the benign god Tishtrya, bringer of gentle rain and fertility. At the start of their grim battle, Apaosa threw down Tishtrya because insufficient prayers, praise, and votive offerings had been made to the good god, but Ohrmazd himself intervened and gave Tishtrya a generous portion of his own divine power. This gift empowered Tishtrya with an enormous surge of strength and he defeated Apaosa. Gentle rain fell, the crops grew, and people were saved. In this legendary battle between two aspects of good and evil represented by Tishtrya and Apaosa, the whole underlying theological concept of dualism can be seen yet again.

There was also a profound belief in demonesses as well as demons like Apaosa in the ancient Middle Eastern culture. Agas, known as "Agas of the evil eye," was a demoness who delighted in causing illness and injury, and there were many others who were equally as bad. The demoness Patierah, for example, was associated with sexual temptation, vice, and infidelity, and more importantly the unhappiness that accompanied them. Allatum, also known as Ellat, was the goddess of the underworld in ancient Persian culture, and although not especially evil, her association with death and the kingdom of gloom, shadow, and darkness made her a being to be feared and placated whenever possible. In much the same category is the demoness of hunger, famine, and starvation — the female counterpart of Apaosa — named Tawrich.

Just as hunger is personified in Tawrich, so the aging process is personified in another very unwelcome demoness — Zarich.

The Persian demon of death — called "he from whom none escape" — is known as Asto Vidatu. His equally feared and loathed companion is Dahaka, not merely another death-demon but a demon responsible for lies, deceit, and treachery, as well. Less sinister, but equally negative and unpleasant is the demon of sloth and laziness, known as Bushyasta. He is described as being sallow and pallid in appearance, and of an unhealthy yellowish colour. His mischievous purpose is to prevent people from doing their essential duties — especially their religious duties — and getting their important work completed.

The serpentine demon-monster that steals cattle and generally does whatever he can to harm human beings is Azhi Dahak, sometimes referred to as "the dragon." He has three heads and six eyes and frequently causes storms that damage flocks, herds, and crops.

To what extent, then, can it be argued that Satanism had at least a few of its roots in the Middle East? Dualism suggests that good and evil — like chaos and order — are diametrically opposed. Where there is belief in such theological, ethical, and philosophical opposites, human beings will tend to see themselves as members of one camp or the other. Where the God of Goodness — by whatever name he is called — leads those who hope that their efforts will make the world a better, happier place for themselves and others, the forces of evil led by Satan, Lucifer, or Ahriman fight against them.

In most ancient Middle Eastern cultures, the things that spoiled life — storms, droughts, famine, illness, injury, mendacity, lies, and treachery — became personified as demons and demonesses, the followers of the evil Ahriman. Gentle rain, fertility, health, loyalty, and truth were also personified as followers of Ohrmazd. These beliefs formed the core of many ancient Middle Eastern religious cultures. The ideas were there, and many things within those ideas provided fruitful ground in which the later concept of Satanism could grow. Ideas tend to spread with traders, and the Phoenicians were prodigious travellers, traders, and colonizers. Wherever they went they carried their gods and demons with them. It did not take too great an effort to identify Ahriman and his evil minions with Satan and his fallen angels from the Abrahamic religions.

Magic, alchemy, necromancy, curses, and spells soon began to form the trappings and accoutrements of the ideas about demons that poured from ancient Persia. These things offered power. The man or woman to whom Ahriman and his demons offered the power to work magic would feel that this was a shortcut to earthly success. If the worship of Ahriman, lord of evil, was the price of such magical power — so what? If an evil advantage is there to be taken — take it!

As the ancient Persian beliefs spread from the Middle East across North Africa and on into Spain, so the worship of Baal, Ashtart, Ahriman, Melqart, and a host of other supposed paranormal entities spread within it. The worship of Ahriman, Baal, and the others may conceivably have been one of the roots from which Satanism grew.

4
Satanism in Ancient Egypt

Archaeological records suggest that the earliest occupants of Egypt were living along the Nile Valley about twenty thousand years ago and subsisting as Stone Age hunter-gatherers. They were nomadic, and their tools and rock carvings have been found in widely separated oases as well as along the banks of the Nile.

Some fifteen thousand years ago, however, things were changing. Early forms of grain-grinding had been discovered, fishing and hunting were augmenting the people's diets, and domestication of cattle was developing. Millennia passed and the climate began to change: the former fertile lands of North Africa slowly gave way to the Sahara Desert. People began moving closer to the Nile in order to survive. Culture became centralized and agricultural. Large buildings first began to appear in Ancient Egypt about eight thousand years ago.

The Naqada culture formed an important reference point for Egyptologists and archaeologists studying this pre-dynastic society in depth. Naqada, on the west bank of the Nile, was not far from the old Egyptian gold mines and was, therefore, known in ancient times as Nubt (meaning "gold"). It was also called Ombos in antiquity.

Professor Sir William Matthew Flinders Petrie (1853–1942), rightly acknowledged to be one of the greatest of the Egyptologists, first examined the Naqada site in 1894 and discovered many significant artifacts there, along with charcoal from the local tombs, later identified as having come from the cedars of Lebanon. These cedars were also associated with King Hiram, who incorporated Lebanese cedar into the refurbishment of the ancient Middle Eastern temples.

One of the earliest dynastic tombs was found close to Naqada at the end of the nineteenth century. It yielded tablets of ivory, clay sealing material, and broken vases. The names of Pharaoh Hor Aha and his wife

Nithotep were inscribed there, but the tomb appeared to have belonged to one of the pharaoh's local government officers responsible for the Naqada area.

What makes Naqada particularly important and relevant for the study of possible roots of Satanism in ancient Egypt is the presence there of a temple dedicated to Seth. In Egyptian mythology, Nut, the beautiful sky goddess, was married to Ra, the king of the gods. She fell in love with Geb, god of the Earth, and this infuriated her husband. He declared that she should not give birth on any of the 360 days of the year as it then was in the ancient Egyptian calendar. Nut went to the very wise god, Thoth, alias Hermes Trismegistus, alias Melchizedek, and asked him for help.

Thoth duly created five extra days by taking light from the moon with which to create them, and it was on these five days that Nut's children (Osiris, Seth, Isis, and Nephthys) were duly born. Osiris was the eldest, and Seth, his brother, was bitterly jealous of him and hated him. Seth is referred to as the god of disorder and chaos, creator of misfortune and danger. He was believed to be responsible for thunder, and for making fertile lands into wildernesses. The worst interpretations of Seth make him into the personification of evil, an arch-fiend equivalent to the devil. The height of his evil was the murder of his brother Osiris, whom he drowned and then dismembered.

Osiris's valiant son, Horus, finally avenged his father. Seth's final fate varies according to the differing myths and legends of Horus's revenge — but there is enough material relating to Seth's *survival* to envisage him as the central figure of a satanic cult. The elements of this Seth worship could well have spread over a very wide area and formed one of the foundations of Satanism.

The Greeks referred to Seth as Typhon and characterized him as a powerful god, one who was feared and held in awe. Various inscriptions gave him titles such as "The Strong One of Thebes" and "He Who Rules the South." His burning arrows were fatal, and he was regarded as the harbinger of death. It was also believed that his bones were iron. Some authorities included the griffin among his entourage.

Egyptian deities were often shown as part-animal, part-human. Frequently the head of an animal or bird was placed on a human body.

Horus, the Avenger, with his hawk.

Pictures of Seth tended to emphasize his long ears with square tips, and his very long, protruding nose. Certain representations give him the appearance of a unicorn or rhinoceros! He was also believed to have resembled an aardvark.

Seth, like almost all of the ancient Egyptian deities, was thought to have a female aspect as well as a male one, but in some versions of the mythology he had a female consort called Taour/Taourt. To the Greeks she was known as Theouris, and was thought to resemble a hybrid of hippopotamus and crocodile.

Lucius Mestrius Plutarchus, the historian, who lived from A.D. 46-120, regarded Seth as the destroyer of life — both plants and animals — and classified him as the direct opponent of Osiris, whom he saw as the giver and sustainer of life and fertility. Seth was seen in the setting (the failure) of the sun and the waning of the moon. He was also regarded as a war god, and a temple was erected to him in that role in Tanis, a town situated in the delta, which was believed to have been a centre of power for the Hyksos, the so-called Shepherd Kings, who were thought to have been involved with Joseph and the arrival of the Hebrews in Egypt.

Pharaoh Sety I seems to have been so-named because he was a worshipper of Seth. The worship of Seth also seems to have extended to the Hittites, among whom he was referred to as Sutech.

The pre-dynastic period in Ancient Egypt ended approximately five thousand years ago, at a time when Egypt was divided into Ta Shemau (the southern part, referred to as Upper Egypt) and Ta Mehu (the northern part, referred to as Lower Egypt). The boundary between them was roughly where modern Cairo is situated.

The first of the dynastic rulers was Narmer, and he has been immortalized by the discovery of the so-called Narmer Palette, which is also referred to as Hierakonpolis Palette. It is believed that this remarkable palette was used to grind the special cosmetics — of which the ancient Egyptians were prolific users — to adorn the statues of their gods. One side of the Narmer Palette shows the king wearing the white crown of Upper Egypt; the other side shows him wearing the red crown of Lower Egypt. The Narmer Palette is also of great archaeological value because it is one of the earliest objects bearing hieroglyphics.

Is it connected in any way with the evil brutality of Seth? The carving *seems* to show a prisoner being put to death by having his skull pierced — but is it also possible that it represents early Egyptian *brain surgery*? Is it a patient being healed rather than an enemy being executed? Another widely accepted interpretation of the carving is that Horus, in the form

The Narmer Palette: military triumph, an execution, or brain surgery?

of a falcon, is shown delivering six thousand captives to the triumphant Narmer, who is not in the act of killing his opponent, nor of performing early Egyptian brain surgery, but is merely brandishing his mace to demonstrate his superiority.

The ancient Egyptian myths and legends concerning Seth do not always cast him in a totally evil role, and this can be seen to have its parallel in the references to Satan in the Abrahamic religions. As already noted in an earlier chapter, in the book of Job, Satan is referred to as *the* Satan — implying that the word *Satan* referred to a rank, or office, rather than to an individual entity. He can be understood as counsel for the prosecution, an interrogator or tester, acting as a means of ascertaining the quality of a human being.

Rather than being the consort of Taour, Seth is married to his sister Nephthys in some versions of the legend — but not in all of them. Nephthys certainly plays no part in the murder of Osiris; in fact, she assists Isis in retrieving the scattered pieces of Osiris in order to facilitate his resurrection.

Another possible root of Satanism from ancient Egypt is the jackal-headed figure of the god Anubis, son of Seth and Nephthys, according to some of the myths. Also known as Inpu, the sinister Anubis is associated with death, mummification, and the afterlife. The leader of a team of embalmers would frequently dress in an Anubis costume when there was a funerary procession. Anubis's relevance for funerals and the embalming process also gives him a function as a tomb guardian, and he is sometimes referred to as "the one who presides over embalming."

Anubis's wife, Anput, accompanies him and assists in his duties. In Egyptian, her name is simply the feminine form of Inpu. It is almost as if they were one and the same god with a feminine and masculine perspective. Their daughter, Kebechet, is the goddess of purity and the purification process. When the Egyptian death rituals are seen symbolizing purification in preparation for life-after-death, the three of them can be seen working together. This aspect of Anubis as a god of death and embalming makes him awesome and frightening rather than evil, but it also invokes the association of death and judgment on the threshold of the afterlife.

There is a nexus here with the Abrahamic religious ideas of life in Paradise for those deemed worthy, and life in Hades, Hell, or Gehenna for those who have lived evil lives. It also ties in with the Faust-type stories of those who have sold their souls to the devil in return for the restoration of their youth and a few extra years of earthly pleasure, but who are dragged away to damnation when those bonus years have elapsed.

Anubis, Guardian of the Dead.

Anubis was often depicted with the head of a jackal because of the scavenging jackal's association with burial places. The jackal would dig up and eat the flesh of the dead when it got the opportunity. Anubis's traditional black colour represented the dark soil in which the dead were buried, and the grim blackness of decaying human flesh.

As time passed and Greek culture became mixed with Egyptian myths and legends, Anubis and Hermes (messenger-god of the Greek pantheon) merged into Hermanubis. Their worship under this name went as far as Rome, and was centred in Uten-ha, known in Greek as Cynopolis, the Town of Dogs. Some roots of Satanism may, perhaps, be traced back to ancient Egypt through this Hermanubis cult because the name Hermanubis crops up occasionally in medieval alchemical literature.

Satanism and demonology are frequently characterized by the phenomenon of curses, and curses have also played a significant part in the belief systems of ancient Egypt. Anubis, for example, is connected with the legendary mummy's curse associated with the Tomb of Tutankhamen, which was opened by Lord Carnarvon and Egyptologist Howard Carter in 1922.

After many frustrating years of searching, Howard Carter discovered the tomb of Tutankhamen in the Valley of the Kings at Luxor on the west bank of the Nile. The story of the alleged curse on the tomb was stimulated by a report that Howard Carter's pet canary was swallowed by a cobra on the day the tomb was found. The cobra is associated with the Egyptian goddess Wadjet, traditional protectress of the Pharaoh, ready to strike at his enemies — should he be threatened in life or in death.

The story of the curse gathered momentum when Lord Carnarvon, who had financed Howard Carter's excavations, died on April 5, 1923. The curse was alleged to have read: "Death comes on swift wings to him who desecrates my tomb." Carnarvon was bitten by a mosquito in February and inadvertently aggravated the bite by cutting it while shaving. Blood poisoning developed, and this led to a bout of pneumonia, which proved fatal.

It should be noted, however, that the exact details of the alleged curse supposedly found in the tomb may have owed more to imaginative journalism than to anything actually inscribed there. It is also important to note in connection with Carnarvon's death that he had suffered severe chest injuries in a motoring accident in Bad Schwalbach in Germany in 1901. This had left him with chronic breathing difficulties for over twenty years, and he had been advised on medical grounds to spend time in warm climates. His medical trips included Egypt, and while there he developed the interest in Egyptology and archaeology that was eventually to prove fatal for him.

Just as the story of the curse was reinforced by the episode of the cobra and Howard Carter's canary, it was also reported that Lord Carnarvon's dog, a fox terrier called Susan, howled and died at the same time as her master passed away! A further factor that added to the melodrama of the curse story was a power failure that cut out all the lights in Cairo for a few minutes just as Lord Carnarvon drew his last breath. Such power failures were by no means uncommon in Cairo in 1923, but this one happened right on cue as far as the curse was concerned!

Howard Carter himself died of lymphoma in March 1939. He was then sixty-four years old. Just as the story of Carnarvon's pet dog and the power-cut in Cairo had synchronized with Carnarvon's death, so a strange story circulated in connection with Carter's death. It was said that among the many treasures and artifacts in Tutankhamen's tomb was an ancient Egyptian trumpet that no one had attempted to blow since the tomb was opened. Apparently, at the precise moment of Carter's death, *someone blew that trumpet!*

When author Lionel was a teacher at Gamlingay Village College in Cambridgeshire in the 1940s, one of his responsibilities was to find interesting and unusual lecturers for a series of general interest talks called "The Thursday Lectures." One of the guest speakers was Richard Adamson, a guard who had actually slept in the tomb of Tutankhamen for weeks as part of his security duties at the time of the excavations. Richard was in excellent health when we met him, and he lived to be well over eighty. In the course of his lecture, he expressed the opinion that Howard Carter had started the legend of the mummy's curse to discourage grave robbers and other possible intruders from visiting the newly found tomb.

Another ancient Egyptian deity associated with evil was Apep. The Greeks referred to him as Apophis. He personified darkness and disorder, chaos and gloom. He was the enemy of light, truth, and order. Usually depicted as an enormous snake, Apep could also appear as a crocodile or a type of dragon. He was said to be fifteen metres long and to have a head that was as hard as flint.

There are several scholarly disagreements over the disturbed period of ancient Egyptian history when the Hyksos were in power. Some have referred to these invaders as the "Shepherd Kings," but this is not generally regarded as the best description of them. Essentially, for a period of some two hundred years or more, the Hyksos dynasty ruled Egypt. It is *possible* that when Joseph arrived as a slave and then rose to power and prominence in Egypt, it was a Hyksos pharaoh who welcomed him, and at the time of Moses and the Exodus, when the Hyksos had lost power to indigenous Egyptians, the unfriendly pharaoh "who knew not Joseph" was Ahmose. What is of particular relevance is that when the Hyksos arrived in Egypt they adopted the worship of Seth, and it was not until they were overthrown that Seth became associated with evil. The indigenous Egyptians apparently turned against Seth, and made him an evil deity, because their enemies, the Hyksos, had favoured him.

Historians of religion and folklore have advanced a general theory that when conquests and occupations take place, the gods of the conquered peoples tend to become the demons of the new religion imposed by the conquerors. This may well have been the case as far as Seth was concerned in ancient Egypt.

After Seth became the focus of evil in Egyptian mythology, Apep fell into second place as an evil entity. Prominence as the master of evil now devolved on Seth, so, fearsome as Apep's appearance was, he became a mere shadow of his former self.

Another particularly fierce and evil Egyptian god was Shesmu. In his more positive aspects he was a god of wine and oil presses. In his horrific and brutal aspects he would tear the head off an evildoer and crush it as if it were a grape in his wine press! One of his titles was "Executioner of the Damned," and he seemed to revel in it and perform those duties with alacrity. His ferocity led to him being represented as a powerful male human figure with the head of a lion.

His consort was Sekhmet, known to the Greeks as Sacmis, a warrior goddess who also had the head of a lion. So fierce was she that it was generally believed by the Egyptians that her burning breath created deserts. Her great responsibility was to protect the pharaohs and lead them into battle. The other warrior goddess was Bast, meaning "the cat," but Sekhmet the lioness was felt to be far more powerful than Bast. In some of the myths, the fierce Sekhmet is regarded as the daughter of Ra, the sun-god, from whom her great strength and hot, destructive breath is drawn. She destroys her enemies with arrows of fire and is accordingly known as "The Woman of Flame." Although not evil in the sense of being malignant and wishing deliberate harm to human beings, Sekhmet's dangerous ferocity as the consort of Shesmu kept the Egyptians in awe of her.

There is a sense in which her ferocity – and the extreme danger of crossing her inadvertently and thus incurring her fatal wrath – puts her in parallel with Lilith, at least in some of the Lilith legends. The Middle Eastern screech-owl, vampire-goddess Lilith was always seen as fierce and vengeful – added to which she was markedly malign, and delighted in human suffering as a way to revenge herself on Adam and all his kin.

Another connection between ancient Egypt, Satanism, and black magic is the mysterious Aleister Crowley.

In 1903, Aleister Crowley married Rose Kelly and they went to Egypt on honeymoon. The following year they went there again, and Rose began experiencing peculiar psychic trances during which she was convinced that the Egyptian god Horus was trying to contact her husband. As Rose had not previously expressed much interest in paranormal phenomena, Crowley took her to the Boulak Museum in Cairo and asked her to point out Horus. She stopped in front of a painted wooden funerary stele of the 26th dynasty depicting a priest named Ankh-efen-Khonsu in the act of holding an offering to Horus. Crowley was amazed to see that the catalogue number on the stele was 666. He thought of himself as 666, the Number of the Beast in the book of Revelation, Chapter 13, verses 17 and 18:

And that no man might buy or sell, save he that had the mark, or the name of the beast, or the number of his name. Here is wisdom. Let him that hath understanding count the number of the beast: for it is the number of a man; and his number is Six hundred threescore and six.

Having the attitude to life and the paranormal that he did, Crowley took the experience in the museum as a sign, and shortly afterward, on March 20, he thought that he was in communication with Horus. He then began referring to his wife as Ouarda the Seeress. Crowley was convinced on April 8 that some supernatural presence was dictating to him from behind his left shoulder and he began writing down what he thought he heard. According to Crowley, the entity that owned the mysterious voice that was dictating to him called itself Aiwass. Aiwass said that he was a messenger from an ancient Egyptian god named Hoor-Paar-Kraat, implying that he was sent by Horus, son of Isis and Osiris. For the next few days Crowley wrote down everything that the strange voice told him, and published the writings later as *The Book of the Law*. The voice told Crowley that he was to be the Prophet of the New Aeon, and that the core of its moral precepts would be: Do what thou wilt shall be the whole of the law.

There were those who were close to Crowley, especially his secretary, Israel Regardie, who were of the opinion that the voice calling itself Aiwass was really a

Aleister Crowley, the Black Magician (1875–1947).

product of Crowley's subconscious mind. Wherever it came from, it linked Crowley's version of what might be termed Satanism to ancient Egyptian roots.

5
Satanism in the Dark Ages

The Dark Ages are popularly regarded as the period between the fall of the Roman Empire and rise of European Christendom under its Holy Roman Emperors. It was a period during which Roman civilization and culture in Britain were shrinking in the face of the indigenous influences, and the arrival of various invaders and immigrants.

Much of Britain had been part of the Roman Empire between the years A.D. 43 and A.D. 410, and was then referred to as Britannia by the Romans. That occupation had meant the arrival and dissemination in Britain of Roman religious beliefs and superstitions from Roman Legionaries who arrived from across the sea.

One of the demons that the Legionaries may well have brought with them to Britain — and which stayed in British mythology long after the Roman Empire fell — was Orcus, god of the underworld and punisher of evildoers. It is believed that there was a temple dedicated to Orcus on the Palatine Hill in Rome, and pictures of him as a hairy giant can be found in Etruscan tombs. Is it possible that the Cerne Abbas Giant in Dorset, England, was a representation of Orcus?

Orcus was more widely worshipped in rural areas, where belief in him seems to have survived throughout the Dark Ages and for centuries after. He also became the central character in the traditional European wild man festivals.

The word *orco*, as distinct from the god's actual name, came to mean a demon or flesh-eating monster, especially in Italy — a creature that was part of Satan's forces. It is also probable that the word *ogre* comes from the same etymological root. Tolkien may well have gone to the same early word-source when deciding to use the word *orcs* for the evil beings in his Lord of the Rings trilogy.

Belief in Orcus, and bloodcurdling tales of the punishments that he handed out after death to oath-breakers, could well have contributed to Satanism in the Dark Ages.

Before the Romans arrived, however, Britain was already trading with Europe, and British tin in particular was being exported far and wide. Wherever traders came and went, they carried ideas as well as goods and services. Prior to the arrival of Roman religious beliefs, Britain and much of Europe were influenced by Celtic thought and Druidism. There was also a powerful Celtic dimension to the mysteries of Rennes-le-Château in southwestern France, mysteries which rank among the most tantalizing enigmas of all time and are thought by some researchers to have a weird, magical dimension. It is possible that some of the sinister secrets associated with Rennes go back to the Dark Ages — or even earlier.

The Tectosages, who lived in and around Toulouse and Rennes in pre-Roman times, were part of a bigger Celtic nation referred to as the Volcae. They were free, independent, and very powerful during the second century B.C. They occupied the area bounded by the Cévennes Mountains and the Garonne and Rhône rivers. Their territory was later known as the Languedoc.

During the nineteenth century, a scholarly priest named Henri Jean-Jacques Boudet (1837–1915) held the parish of Rennes-les-Bains, not far from Bérenger Saunière's parish of Rennes-le-Château. Boudet made a particular study of the mysterious Celtic language and an equally mysterious Celtic cromlech, or dolmen stone, in his parish. He wrote an enigmatic book about it, called *La Vraie Langue Celtique et le Cromleck de Rennes-les-Bains*.

Boudet's grave in the cemetery at Axat, in southern France, has a mysterious stone carving of a book on it. The inscription on that stone book may refer to a page number in Boudet's book and that page may hold a vital clue to the Rennes-le-Château mystery.

The last hundred copies seem to have been destroyed in 1914 on the orders of a querulous, interfering, and unpleasantly bureaucratic bishop named de Beauséjour, who also made himself a profound nuisance to Bérenger Saunière.

Like all Celts, the Tectosages of southwestern France seem to have had a form of religion that was animistic: a belief that mountains, rivers, trees, rocks, and stones — such as the cromlech of Rennes-les-Bains — all possessed spirits, some of which were evil and hostile. This veneration of stones included a particular interest in stones that had holes through them. These often formed part of Celtic burial sites, and it was thought that the holes were intended to aid the escape of the spirit of the dead. It was also suggested that when a Celtic priest or magician wanted to obtain revelations from the spirit world, he would "listen" at the hole in the sacred stone.

Much Celtic religion involved Druids and Druidism. It was suppressed by the Romans as their power and influence spread, but managed to survive longer in Britain than in the Roman provinces of Europe. Druids were not only Celtic priests, but were found in other parts of Celtic society, as well.

Georges Dumézil, a celebrated French mythographer (1898-1986), put forward a hypothesis that divided ancient societies into three functional groups: religious leaders, fighters, and everyone else. The three groups respectively looked after: sacred, philosophical, and intellectual affairs; warfare and defence; and economic and agricultural matters. The work of the Druids extended beyond the purely spiritual priestly functions and included seers, bards, judges, and teachers. Druids believed in reincarnation, and revered the oak and mistletoe, incorporating them into their religious rites. Druidism flourished, particularly on what was then called the Island of Mona (Anglesey in North Wales), where there were special sacred groves. These were eventually hacked down by the Romans on the orders of Claudius.

There were other important religious sites in Britain, as well. The old pre-Roman British goddess Ancasta, for example, had a shrine at Bitterne, near Southampton, and may well have been the goddess associated with the River Itchen in accordance with Druidic animism.

Frequently, a local British god would get amalgamated with a Roman god during the occupation prior to the onset of the Dark Ages. One such example of this occurring was at Mars Rigonemetos at Nettleham in Lincolnshire in England. The Celtic term *Rigonemetos* translates as "King of the Sacred Grove" and may well have reminded the Roman occupiers of a similar grove at Tiora in central Italy. At Tiora, there was an oracle in the form of a magical woodpecker that answered questions and predicted the future.

These Dark Ages, with their combined Roman and pre-Roman religious beliefs, mythologies, and superstitions, provided fruitful soil in which the seeds of Satanism flourished.

Early Christianity condemned paganism, and regarded the old nature gods and the animistic spirits of rivers and trees as demons. Celtic Druidism, with its belief in animism and reincarnation, fought to survive.

The influence of Anglo-Saxon religion and belief in the Norse gods was also significant during the Dark Ages. The Anglo-Saxon pagans worshipped numerous gods, whom they referred to as *ése*. Woden was king of their pantheon, and was also regarded as the ancestor of most of the Anglo-Saxon royal families. In some of their myths he was leader of the Wild Hunt. There is also an ancient healing spell in Anglo-Saxon history known as the charm of nine herbs, and Woden features prominently in it. Thunor, god of the sky and god of thunder, was another very popular Anglo-Saxon deity who was worshipped by the masses. Woden, in comparison, was venerated by royalty and the aristocracy.

Many centuries before the Nazis misappropriated it, the swastika was Thunor's symbol, as was the battle hammer. Both of these were frequently found on Anglo-Saxon graves. A third Anglo-Saxon god was Tiw, who was identified with the Pole Star.

The pagan Anglo-Saxons were not short of female deities. Frige was their goddess of love; Eostre was a goddess of spring and fertility; Hretha was their goddess of glory, celebration, and triumph. These goddesses shrank to the role of female demons as early Christianity advanced in Britain and Europe.

During the transition years from Anglo-Saxon paganism to Christianity there were occasions on which a compromise enabled *both* forms of religion to be practised within the same building. At the beginning of the seventh century, King Racdwald of East Anglia had been taught the outlines of Christianity, but he had a strong-minded pagan wife who exerted a profound influence over him. He therefore arranged two altars, side by side — one for the worship of Christ, the other for the worship of what his Christian opponents referred to as devils.

During one of many battles in the year 666, a pagan priest was recorded as attempting to curse Christian opponents and to handicap them in battle by means of what the record called "magical arts." That these old pagan Anglo-Saxon magical rites were roundly condemned as Satanism by the Christians is verified by the records of the Second Council of Clofesho/Clovesho, held in 747.

Archbishop Egbert of the council roundly declared that no Christian priest was allowed to practise astrology or enchantment. He also condemned all those who worshipped idols, gave themselves to the devil, or practised divination, auguries, or magical incantations. Egbert's condemnations suggest that a form of Satanism certainly seemed to be flourishing widely in eighth-century Britain!

The pagan Anglo-Saxon belief system also extended to an association of illness and injury with devils, demons, and evil spirits of various types. These malignant entities were thought to be the cause of all kinds of mental and physical problems. An Anglo-Saxon with a contagious fever, or the delusion that invisible wolves and bears were pursuing him, would blame evil spirits.

Another source of Satanism in the Dark Ages was the mythology of the Norse gods and their enemies. The *jotunn* were Scandinavian nature spirits, sometimes gigantic, sometimes of human proportions. Their relationships with the gods were mixed: often they were enemies and the source of much evil, at other times they intermarried with the gods.

This intermarrying goes some way to explaining the very curious Norse god of trouble and mischief, Loki. His consort, the goddess Sygin — whose name translates as "victorious mistress" or "triumphant woman-friend" — stays loyally with him and relieves his suffering when the gods have bound him underneath a poisonous serpent that drips venom on him. Loki's worst evil deed is to cause the death of the god Balder, but he is also responsible for many lesser acts of treachery and betrayal of the gods.

Loki produced three terrible children: the Fenris wolf, the Midgard Serpent, and Hela (Death). It is a relatively simple transition to envisage Loki as a satanic figure during the Dark Ages, and the early church would certainly have seen him in that light.

Another possible source of Satanism and the widespread belief in demons and devils during the Dark Ages was the constant danger in which people lived. Travel was especially hazardous during those centuries. Outlaws were everywhere and would frequently waylay, rob, and kill travellers. There was also constant danger from wild animals. Undertaking a journey in the Dark Ages was an act of real courage — sometimes motivated by religious desires to undertake a pilgrimage. Forests, which were widespread, were filled with highly dangerous brigands and outlaws. Travelling by night, or having to find somewhere to rest overnight, was often the most hazardous part of the journey. The dangers stimulated belief in ghosts, evil spirits, and demons. The fate of neighbours and friends who never reached a planned destination was speculated upon. Had they been bewitched? Had they fallen into the clutches of Satan, or one of his evil minions?

A traditional Dark-Age devil or demon.

Just being a stranger was in itself a danger. If you were in a place where you were *not* a known and trusted family member or tested and reliable friend, you were perceived as a potential threat. A stranger *might* be an innocent traveller, but he might also be a brigand, a cattle rustler, a horse thief, or a kidnapper, hence killing him *might* be a good way to safeguard the village and its inhabitants. As far as villagers were concerned in those dangerous and superstitious times, the unknown traveller *might* be a devil, a demonic shape-shifter, a witch, a wizard, a werebeast, or someone possessed by an evil spirit ... so the widespread fears and uncertainties that characterized the Dark Ages may well have promoted the growth of superstition and, ultimately, Satanism.

The Dark Ages were also times when outstanding Christian missionaries and teachers became lights in the social and intellectual darkness. The struggling new churches paid more attention to biblical references to devils and demons. Various *names* associated with evil entities appear in the Bible: Lucifer, Beelzebub, Belial, Abaddon, and Apollyon.

Some of the devil's *characteristics* are also listed in the holy book, and these would have been noted by Christians fighting for their faith and their lives during the Dark Ages. Matthew's Gospel, for example, in Chapters 4 and 13 describes him as "the tempter" and "the evil one." John's Gospel, Chapter 8, refers to him as "the father of lies." Paul's Second Letter to the Corinthians, Chapter 4, calls him "the god of this world," and Paul's Letter to the Ephesians calls him "the prince of the powers of the air." Revelation, Chapter 12, calls him "the deceiver ... the great dragon" and "the ancient serpent."

A specialized area of paranormal research that is sometimes referred to as Judeo-Christian Demonology provides many other names for demonic entities, and lists some of their duties and characteristics: Abigor, who commands sixty legions of fallen angels; Adramelech, the king of fire; Andras, a bird-headed demon with wings like an angel; Alocer, a demonic horseman with the face of a lion; Balaam, who has three heads; Beelzebub, lord of the flies; Bifrons, a mathematical and astrological demon; and Botis, who has the form of a snake and can foretell the future.

The ancient Sumerian and Babylonian myths concerning demons trickled down into Hebrew traditions, and on into Greco-Roman religious culture. From there, the demon myths followed the Legionaries to the far corners of the Roman Empire. After the Empire's collapse and the arrival of the Dark Ages, it lingered on in places like Britain. Mesopotamian demonology at its earliest and simplest saw demons as the personifications of disease, drought, plagues, flood, and a host of other disasters. In the troubled Dark Ages, it seems likely that demons would be blamed for these things just as they were in ancient Mesopotamia.

Like the Dark Age Christians, the early Mesopotamians felt that they were under continuous attack from a variety of demons, and they defended themselves with the use of magic. Bowls and dishes inscribed with protective words were buried underneath Babylonian houses. The intention was that the marauding demons would be enticed into these bowls and trapped there so that they could not plague the householders. Amulets and other adornments were also inscribed with magical words and symbols to protect their wearers. Dark Age Christians would wear a cross on a chain around the neck, not only to show their allegiance to the church but to drive away evil entities.

During the long years of their captivity, the Hebrews were exposed to Babylonian religious culture and some of this filtered down into later Judeo-Christian thinking. Lilith, for example, the vampire screech-owl demoness who threatened children, may well have had her origins among the Babylonian demon group known as the *lilitu*.

References to Satanism and the devil during the Dark Ages can be found in place names and in legends that set out to explain various local features.

Marston Moretaine, in Bedfordshire, England, contains "the devil's jump stone." According to legend, a farmer was playing leapfrog on the Sabbath when the devil appeared on top of the church tower, leaped down from it, seized the farmer, and carried him off to hell for his sin of Sabbath-breaking. The spot where Satan landed beside the farmer is marked by the stone — actually a geological erratic, less than a metre high, left behind by a receding glacier.

Aldworth in Berkshire, England, is the site of Grim's Ditch, also known as Grim's Bank. The name *Grim* is often used to indicate Satan, although it may be related to the Anglo-Saxon word *grimr*, which translates as "hooded."

The Devil's Dyke near Brighton, in East Sussex, is another natural geological feature that was formed by meltwater at the end of the last British ice age. It is a steep-sided V-profiled valley near the village of Poynings on the north face of the South Downs. According to legend, the devil was furiously angry because the local pagans had converted to Christianity, so he began work on the dyke to drown them all. Working by night, according to tradition, he had to complete the dyke and fly back to hell before morning. Fortunately for the locals, an old woman suffering from insomnia lit a candle beside her cottage window well before dawn, and the light disturbed her rooster, which thought it *was* dawn and crowed loudly. Afraid that it was really daybreak, the devil stopped work and the planned flooding never took place. There are many "Devil's Dykes" scattered throughout Britain. One is near Gallows Hill in Burwell in Cambridgeshire, and another, the massive Cambridgeshire Devil's Dyke, nearly thirteen kilometres long, runs from Reach to Woodditton.

Another interesting devil legend from the Dark Ages concerns Batcombe Down Cross in Dorset, which is also known as Cross Hand Stone. Within two kilometres of the village stands this short stone pillar with a hand carved on it. The legend says that the priest of Batcombe, a sincere and courageous man, set out through a violent storm to take the sacrament to a dying parishioner. When he reached the dying man's home, he found that somewhere along the way he had dropped the pyx containing the holy sacrament. Fearlessly setting out again through the stormy darkness to look for the pyx, he was amazed to see a pillar of fire rising steadily skyward, completely unaffected by the ferocious wind and rain. He was even more astonished to see a ring of cattle kneeling around the pillar of flame and worshipping his missing pyx at its base. Among the kneeling cattle was a sinister-looking black horse that was down on one knee only, whereas the cattle knelt reverently on both knees. The priest challenged the horse as to why it was not kneeling fully like the cattle. The horse — actually Satan — answered that it would not kneel at all if it had the power to resist the holy sacrament. The priest then asked why the devil had assumed the form of a horse.

"In order that men may attempt to steal me — and then be hanged for their sins, and come down to my infernal realms!" answered the horse.

The priest retrieved his pyx and returned to the dying man's home to administer the sacrament to him. The Cross Hand Stone was erected to commemorate this Dark Age miracle.

Another devil's place name can be found in Tunstall, in Norfolk. It is associated with the loss of the bells from the now-ruined church of St. Peter and St. Paul. It is said that when a fire destroyed it centuries ago, there were quarrels as to what was to be done with the bells, which had miraculously escaped damage. While the argument was going on, Satan settled it by snatching the bells and running away with them. The local priest pursued him courageously, chanting a Latin exorcism as he ran. Terrified by the exorcism, Satan opened the Earth and dived in, taking a shortcut back to hell and carrying the bells with him. The place where this happened has since developed into a marshy water pool known as Hell Hole. A group of alder trees beside the water is known as Hell Carr. The legend is perpetuated by a stream of bubbles that disturb the water in Hell Hole. Although the bubbles are almost certainly the simple result of marsh gas, the legend alleges that the bubbles are caused by the still-descending bells into the bottomless pit.

Another Dark Age legend tells of the devil's treasure in the depths of Callow Pit near Southwood Road, where the parishes of Moulton St. Mary and Cantley meet. Two impoverished villagers from Southwood attempted to take the devil's treasure from the pit. After much struggling, they got a hook through the handle. They were retrieving the treasure when a great satanic claw came up through the water and began pulling the treasure chest down again into the stygian depths of the pit. Despite all their heroic struggles, the chest was torn from their grasp and they were left only with the handle. For many years this handle adorned the door of the town's St. Edmund's Church.

Somerset provides the legend of yet another contest between a fearless priest and Satan. The site known as Tarr Steps crosses the River Barle on Exmoor. According to legend, the devil built it in a single night, having carried the necessary stones in his apron. Satan vowed that no one else would ever be able to cross this causeway that he had constructed. He swore that anyone who attempted to cross Tarr Steps would be torn limb from limb. The villagers sent a cat over first, and the unfortunate feline was killed by the devil. The fearless local priest went across next and challenged Satan to injure him. The devil met him halfway but was powerless to harm him, and the priest began reciting a Latin exorcism. The devil retaliated by cursing the priest, but this failed to weaken the exorcism. The satanic curses did, however, affect the surrounding trees, which wilted. Finally, the valiant priest succeeded and the devil fled, leaving it safe for all to cross Tarr Steps.

Satan was sometimes referred to as a dragon, and dragons from the Dark Ages were particularly sinister and malicious beasts. The myths of Greco-Roman and Middle Eastern chthonic dragons and monsters — those which were thought to inhabit the underworld — blended with the European Dark Age dragons. The legendary creatures that emerged from this hybridization were more terrible than any of their mythical ancestors.

Stories of multi-headed dragons and serpents that terrified Europe in the Dark Ages owed something of their pedigree to the Lernaean Hydra that Hercules killed as one of his twelve labours. Beneath the waters of Lake Lerna was purported to be the Hydra's den and an entrance to the Underworld that the Hydra guarded.

The mythological tree Yggdrasil is said to have had one of its roots in Niflheim — the lair of terrifying dragons. One Persian dragon, Abraxas, seems to have been carried far and wide by some of the Roman Legionaries who were soaked in Middle Eastern mythology. Abraxas, who was regarded as a form of Satan by some Dark Age thinkers, had the head of a gigantic cockerel (rooster), the body of a huge serpent, and two great legs ending in talons. He was reputedly very powerful, but also savagely ill-tempered, which made him particularly dangerous.

Another dragon legend that eventually reached Western Europe as the Roman Empire spread toward Britain concerned Zu, who was also known as Anzu. She was a particularly crafty and cunning female dragon, and the element of guile and treachery in her nature was thought of as particularly satanic. According to the original Sumerian legend of Zu, she stole the priceless tablets of the law, which were known as the Tupsimati, and hid them in her nest in the mountains. In the original Sumerian version of the legend, Ninerta, the good and powerful sun god, killed Zu and brought the tablets back so that the order of the universe could continue. The Europeanized Dark Age versions of the legend tended to leave out the death of Zu and the restoration of the tablets of the law. In

Variations on the theme of multi-headed monsters in the Dark Ages.

the lawless, chaotic Dark Ages it was all too easy to believe that the tablets were missing again. Had Zu been resurrected and stolen them again? Or had one of her children done it? Different versions of the Zu legend describe her as having a lion's body and an eagle's head. Other accounts give her a humanoid body with an eagle's wings and powers of flight.

The dragon of Aller, a town near Langport in Somerset, was a truly terrifying and demonic beast according to legend. It had huge leathery wings, and spat fire and flame in the traditional dragon manner. It was a creature that was synonymous with destruction and ruined the fertile land for kilometres around Aller. In one version of the legend, a hero named John of Aller was able to kill it after a tremendous battle that almost cost him his life. In other versions it survived and remains hidden in its cave not far from Langport. As with the legend of Zu, the Aller dragon has supposedly left its offspring behind to grow up and terrorize the land again.

Cawthorne Well in Yorkshire was the supposed home of a legendary flying dragon that was disturbed when water was drawn from the well. It emerged and flew to nearby Cawthorne Park. As water was traditionally associated with important religious practices such as baptism, and the sprinkling of holy water that had been blessed as part of the exorcism ritual, the devil in the form of a dragon would be thought to want to discourage villagers from drawing water.

Deerhurst, near Tewkesbury in Gloucestershire, also has a Dark Age legend of a fierce, dangerous, and evil dragon — a satanic creature that ate cattle and spread deadly poison wherever it went. A generous reward consisting of many acres of good fertile land was offered to anyone who would kill the dragon, but for a long time nobody volunteered because the beast was exceptionally dangerous. Finally, John, a muscular blacksmith, thought of a plan. He prepared a great trough of milk, which he thought the dragon would find good to drink. He was right. The dragon drank so much that it became sleepy and finally dozed off beside the empty trough. Using every ounce of his hardened blacksmith's muscle, John crept up to the sleeping dragon and brought his axe down across its neck, decapitating it. He was duly given his reward, and there is talk that his descendants still farm those acres that their ancestor's strength and courage won for them.

The famous saga of Beowulf belongs to the Dark Ages, as well, and sheds very interesting light on the relationship between myths of dangerous dragons and monsters and the growth of Satanism during those centuries. An important theme in *Beowulf* is the persistence and recurrence in different forms of the dragon, the demon – a monster of one sort or another that brings death and disaster to humans. Another significant theme is the sacrifice that the hero makes in overcoming the evil entity that threatens the people he is protecting. The saga also emphasizes the importance of courage and loyalty – the essential qualities of those who seek to overcome evil.

In summary, Hrothgar was a Danish king in the sixth century A.D. He and his army occupied a great hall known as Heorot, where they feasted and celebrated. For more than ten years, Grendel, a dangerous and hideous water-dragon, attacked the hall and night after night killed Hrothgar's men. Beowulf, a valiant prince of the Geats from the south of Sweden, heard about what was happening to Hrothgar's men in Denmark and came to their rescue with fourteen of his own Swedish thanes. Reaching Heorot, Beowulf told Hrothgar and his courtiers about the water monsters like Grendel that he had already killed. Instead of the deserved gratitude for coming to their aid, Beowulf was accused of idle boasting and gross exaggeration by one of Hrothgar's men named Unferth. Hrothgar, however, trusts Beowulf and offers him a rich reward if he will slay Grendel. Unferth's foolishness and misjudgement are exposed when Grendel arrives that night. The Danes run for their lives: Beowulf tackles the monster in single combat and so great is Beowulf's strength and courage that he tears off Grendel's arm as they wrestle: the monster retreats to its underwater home where it bleeds to death. The Danes return and are lavish in their praise of Beowulf, who is duly rewarded.

The next problem – the persistence and amplification of evil – is Grendel's mother. Grendel's mother came to Heorot and killed Aeschere, a cherished friend and adviser to Hrothgar. Beowulf sets out after Grendel's mother, a far more dangerous opponent than her son. Beowulf eventually slays her, and takes Grendel's head back to King Hrothgar as a trophy. Beowulf then returns home, but promises to return if Hrothgar ever needs help again.

Many years pass. Beowulf, now an old man, is the good and wise ruler of the Geats in southern Sweden. After a long and happy reign, he is attacked by a dragon — an even more terrible opponent than either Grendel or his mother. With a handful of companions, Beowulf goes in search of the dragon and is determined to fight it in single combat — an essential part of the hero theme. Beowulf's sword breaks and he is severely wounded by the evil beast. All of Beowulf's thanes, except for the truly loyal Wiglaf, run from the dragon and desert Beowulf. Wiglaf risks his life to fight beside Beowulf. He runs through the flames the dragon has created and stabs it: Beowulf then cuts it in half with his knife but realizes that he, himself, is dying. He gives Wiglaf instructions for his funeral and is cremated. His ashes and the dragon's vast treasure are laid to rest in a tomb known as Beowulf's Barrow overlooking the sea.

There is a recurring and increasing power of satanic evil in the *Beowulf* saga revealed in the form of Grendel, Grendel's mother, and, finally, the dragon that brings about the hero's death. There is also the ultimate heroic sacrifice that accompanies the overthrow of this increasingly powerful evil.

Grendel's mother had magical powers, and the Dark Ages were full of witchcraft, wizardry, and black magic. The techniques of that Dark Age magic and the accessories its practitioners used were closely associated with early forms of Satanism.

Medieval Satanism

The power and influence enjoyed by the medieval church led to problems of authoritarianism, repression, and restriction, which many people quite rightly resented. Understandably they were lured back toward Wicca and other old pagan nature religions, which offered freedom from the sexual restrictions that formed a significant part of medieval church teachings.

The conflict between medieval Christianity and the old nature religions was often symbolized dramatically where a Christian church had been built deliberately in the centre of a far older pagan site. An example can be seen at Knowlton in Dorset, where an early Norman church was built in the middle of a prehistoric henge dating back to 2500 B.C.

Knowlton Church in Dorset, England was built in the centre of a prehistoric henge.

Christian teachings in the Middle Ages were strong in Ireland because of the evangelical work of St. Patrick, while St. Columba took them to Scotland and the north of England.

Medieval church teachings about sex tended to be limiting and restrictive in the extreme.

Some of the patristic writers and medieval church leaders were so vehemently opposed to sex — even within marriage — that they didn't bother to provide reasons for forbidding or condemning it. In their jaundiced view, sex was simply so obviously bad, unpleasant, and wrong that it condemned itself. Augustine and his followers, for example, taught that sex presented serious moral dangers simply because strong sexual urges were not under the control of the human will.

John Cassian (A.D. 360-435), also known as John the Ascetic, was one of the Scythian monks, or Desert Fathers, whose ideas were very influential throughout the medieval church. He devised training schemes to help young monks to avoid "the perils of the flesh." Cassian's definitive plans included diet, clothing, posture, and sleeping routines.

Augustine of Hippo (A.D. 354-430) taught that the only proper reason for sex was to produce offspring, and that sex undertaken for pleasure was sinful.

Consequently, the medieval church was a mass of intricate negative sexual rules, regulations, and restrictions. Sex was forbidden during menstruation, pregnancy, and while breastfeeding. No sex was allowed during Lent, Advent, Easter Week, or Whitsun Week. Feast days and fast days had to be sex-free, as did Saturdays and Sundays, Wednesdays, and Fridays. Sex was also forbidden during daylight hours. Fondling and passionate kissing were frowned upon, as were oral sex, anal sex, and imaginative sexual positions. In view of these incredibly ridiculous regulations, it seems close to miraculous that the human race managed to survive at all!

Compared and contrasted with these nonsensical church-imposed restrictions, pagan teachings about sex were open, inviting, and natural.

Unlike Crowley's misinterpretation of the genuine old pagan moral attitude, the central teaching of medieval nature religion was, and still is, "Do what thou wilt — *as long as it harms no one.*"

Crowley's deliberate omission of the conditional clause extracts all the morality from the teaching. Within the proper moral and ethical framework of *harming no one*, the old pagan traditions regard sensuality and sexuality as natural and sacred things to be enjoyed, revered, and celebrated. The ancient pagan faiths acknowledged and accepted human eroticism. There were many pagan love goddesses, fertility goddesses, and sex goddesses. Belief in their existence, and the rituals and liturgies that accompanied such belief, offered a welcome escape from the restrictions that the medieval church imposed.

This desire to escape from the church's prohibitions stimulated a return — often a secretive return — to paganism and the old nature religions. In the eyes of the church, paganism and the old nature religions were evil and satanic, and roundly condemned as such. Some of the followers of the old nature religions turned to witchcraft, wizardry, and sorcery, and these were also vehemently condemned by the medieval church.

At the time, various laws were passed against what was often described as "heathenism." King Athelstan (A.D. 893-939), son of Edward the Elder, passed a law under which the penalty for witchcraft was four months in prison. King Edgar (A.D. 943-975) passed laws making it an offence to "sing heathen songs, to indulge in necromancy, play 'devil-games' and take part in 'well-worshipping.'" The penalty for any of these religious crimes, however, was death.

This medieval church persecution of witches, wizards, sorcerers, necromancers, and magicians in general understandably drove the practitioners into hiding. It was from this persecution and consequent secrecy that medieval Satanism may have grown.

A singularly interesting example of this has been discovered at Glozel, near Vichy, in central France. During the 1920s, a cow belonging to the Fradin family who farmed at Glozel fell into a deep hole about three metres long and a couple of metres wide. Teenager Emile Fradin went down into the hole to put webbing under the cow so that his grandfather and a group of strong friends and neighbours could ease her up to the surface again. The rescue was a success, and the puzzled cow, none the worse for her misadventure, wandered off to continue her grazing.

Young Emile, however, asked his grandfather's permission to stay and examine the contents of the hole, which contained a number of storage niches and alcoves that held ancient clay tablets engraved with an unknown alphabet, carved bones and antlers, flint axes and arrowheads, and strange Stone-Age statuettes. Later investigations concluded that in all probability the hole had originally been a medieval magician's warehouse. When setting out on his rounds, the magician had put a layer of leaves and branches over the store of "magical" objects to disguise it. It was assumed that one day the magician had fallen afoul of the Inquisition and had been executed. Over the centuries, nature took its course, and the top of the hole became indistinguishable from the surrounding grazing land, leading to the incident with the Fradins' cow and young Emile's discoveries. The authors made a firsthand investigation of the site in 1975, when Lionel was lecturing on the psychology and sociology of unexplained phenomena for Cambridge University's Extra-Mural Board. They met with Emile Fradin, who had made the discoveries when a teenager, and were able to discuss his finds in detail.

Medieval witchcraft was regarded both by its practitioners and their opponents as the use of supernatural, paranormal, or magical powers. The medieval church opposed witchcraft so vehemently because it believed that the powers witches possessed came from Satan and his fallen angels. In a pre-scientific society, with a superstitious culture, witchcraft and magic became ways of explaining events that were not otherwise understandable, such as the inexplicable sickness or death of a person or an animal, or natural phenomena such as violent storms, fires, or floods. In medieval Europe, and especially in the Germanic Territories, witchcraft was thought to be a vast, coordinated conspiracy against Christianity and the church. This belief led to witch-hunts and the torture and execution of those who confessed.

But what exactly was medieval magic, and how did its practitioners set about their work?

Medieval magic seems to have had *language* at its core. Sometimes the words were spoken aloud; sometimes they went silently through the mind of the magician. Very often the words invoked the devil, or some powerful demon, to aid the magician. Just as the medieval Roman Catholic Church used Latin, so did the medieval magicians and Satanists. The nexus between language and magic may be based on a belief that words themselves may possibly exert some strange kind of influence on the universe. It is certainly true that the use of language to describe events and the environment in which they take place takes the speaker of the words beyond his own immediate personal experiences.

The use of magical words seems to be of greater importance to the witch, wizard, or sorcerer than rituals that are non-verbal. Magical language differs essentially from what might be termed "rational" or "scientific" language in so far as the rational, scientific use of language gives words specific and unambiguous meanings. A star is always a star. The soil is always the soil.

Magical language by contrast is symbolic, emotive, and filled with similes and metaphors. There is also a tendency for magical language to take the form of songs, chants, prayers, and spells rather than normal conversational speech. It frequently reverts to ancient verbal forms, taken from languages of the distant past. Is this, perhaps, an attempt on the part of the magician to get back to some sort of "classical" magical era?

By using strange language forms, the magician also makes the words largely incomprehensible to listeners who are not also magicians. Magic can also be defined as a method of attempting to influence other people – and the environment. It seeks to cause specific effects. Various spells and magical rituals have particular objectives: to affect wealth, health, and emotions such as love. The benign or harmless witch or wizard will attempt to heal, to increase the harvest, or to make people love one another. The malignant witch or wizard will damage crops, flocks, and herds, or attempt to cause illness or hatred among people. It was believed that such negative, malevolent magic owed its origins to Satan and the demons and evil spirits under his control.

There is a significant distinction to be made between magical *knowledge* and the actual power to *perform* magic. It was believed by medieval magicians, sorcerers, and enchanters that magical *knowledge* could be passed down in a family, or via an apprenticeship to a practising magician. Knowing how it was done, however, was distinct from the actual ability to *do* it. Such magical knowledge was normally well-guarded.

To function as an actual magician, however, required *more* than knowledge alone; it was often believed that the magician had to possess some sort of magical equipment as well, such as a wand, a mirror, a crystal ball, a broomstick, or a black cat. The cat was thought of as a "familiar" spirit — a little demon on loan from Satan to the black magician to enable the sorcerer to perform magical acts.

Certain life experiences were believed to indicate the possession of magical power. A magician who had recovered from a near-fatal illness, or who had miraculously survived a near-fatal accident, was thought to be in possession of some strange power that made him an ideal healer.

It seems to be a psychological and sociological truism that a magician's power is derived to a significant extent from what people *believe* about that power. In cases of what appears to be miraculous healing, for example, the psychosomatic element is of major importance. The sick person who knows that the healer who is helping him has already had great therapeutic success with numerous other desperately ill patients over many years will bring his own belief system into effect at a deep subconscious level — and the mind's power over the body is still only partially understood and frequently underrated. The body's own self-healing powers are potentially enormous, if only they can be focused and made to function optimally. A firm *belief* in the powers of the miraculous, magical healer can occasionally be the trigger that the patient's body needs to bring about a wonderful, positive result.

Belief in the magician's power can also work negatively. The victim of a curse who *believes* in the frightening, evil power of the magician who laid the curse is in danger of succumbing to it.

Medieval witches, wizards, and sorcerers who performed magical rituals with what they believed to be the assistance of Satan and various demons, used certain actions along with their magical words.

The brilliant Bronislaw Malinowski (1884-1942), often praised as the father of social anthropology, once described the language used in magical rituals as having "a high coefficient of weirdness." What he meant was that the archaic and extraordinary language used by the magicians in the course of their rituals helped to create an atmosphere that encouraged those present to believe in the efficacy of the ritual. The words, the actions, the postures, the gestures, and the involvement of magical objects all worked together as an inclusive and definitive magical function.

James Frazer (1854-1938), another great social anthropologist, wrote the epoch-making work *The Golden Bough* in which he argued that magic had been replaced by religion, which had in turn been replaced by science. Frazer was of the opinion that there were two basic principles involved in magical symbolism. These were *similarity* and *contagion*. Sympathetic magic encompassing The Law of Similarity infers that that the magician can produce an effect merely by imitating it. This comes into play when the object used by the magician is similar to the object that the magician is trying to affect, such as a voodoo doll in the likeness of an intended victim. Contagious magic was based on the idea that objects that had been in contact with each other would continue to influence each other — using a lock of hair or a stolen personal item to wield power over a target, for example.

Suspicion of magic, and those thought to possess magical powers during the Middle Ages, even extended to such forward-thinking church leaders as Pope Sylvester II, whose papacy ran from 999-1003. Before becoming Pope Sylvester II, Gerbert d'Aurillac (946-1003) had a richly deserved reputation as a scholar, mathematician, and astronomer. Much of his great wisdom and knowledge of mathematics was derived from the Arab world and this led to many malicious rumours to the effect that he was a magician in league with Satan. The main reason for these accusations was his determination to stamp out simony and other corruption in the church. His honesty attracted many enemies in high places.

A very similar case of a pioneering medieval scientist who was suspected of being a magician was Albertus Magnus (*circa* 1200-80). Albertus was Dominican, and a bishop and university teacher. He was a master of the natural sciences, theology, and philosophy, and an expert in mathematics, astronomy, ethics, and metaphysics — not to mention strongly suspected by those who were jealous of him of being a secret magician!

The ideas behind what Frazer had described as contagious magic manifested themselves during the Middle Ages when churches in different locations began competing for the relics of saints in order to attract pilgrims. Saint's relics were believed to have healing powers in accordance with the theories of contagious magic.

An example can be found at Dereham in Norfolk, where the tomb of Saint Withburga, an abbess who gave generously to help the poor, was believed to contain water with healing powers. Withburga was a princess, one of the daughters of King Anna of the East Angles. Her sisters were buried in Ely, and the monks of Ely came to Dereham and stole Withburga's body so that it could be re-interred beside her sisters. There was also the question of attracting pilgrims to Ely rather than to Dereham. After Withburga's body was removed, however, a spring of holy, healing water came up in her tomb, attracting more pilgrims than the saint herself had done!

Another significant dimension of medieval Satanism was the grimoire, a book of magical spells and incantations. The Jewish Kabbalah, a religious book whose title translates from the Hebrew as "that which is being received," deals with the *mystical dimension* of rabbinic Judaism. Its teachings are esoteric. They seek to explain the relationship of a mysterious God, the infinite and eternal Creator and Sustainer, with the finite physical universe. The Kabbalah had a great deal of influence on medieval Christian occultism, and its teachings led to the production of some of the first of the medieval grimoires. These early grimoires dealt with the intricacies of what medieval magicians thought of as demonology and angelology. There was a traditional medieval Christian background to a number of the spells contained in the books. The magician — just like the Christian priest, monk, or friar — went in for fasting, lengthy prayers, and participation in the sacraments. The sacred name of God in Hebrew, Greek, and Latin would then be used to overpower the demons the magician had summoned and force them to do what was wanted: this almost invariably meant satisfying the magician's desire for power, wealth, and sex.

Grimoires contained methods for creating magical tools and equipment, such as talismans and amulets that could be used in spells.

St. Withburga's Tomb in Dereham, Norfolk, England.

They also gave instructions for the precise ways that spells should be performed: what should be said; what should be done with the magical equipment, and what gestures the magician should use.

Rather surprisingly, some grimoires were tolerated. These were the ones that had come down from Anglo-Saxon traditions and contained what was considered to be "nature magic," which was thought to be part of God's creation and, therefore, acceptable. Their main content consisted of spells for healing the sick, along with details of healing herbs. Those grimoires to which the medieval church took the strongest exception were the ones that dealt with demonology, divination, and necromancy.

The Crusades and the Moorish occupation of Spain led to increased contact between Christians and Muslims, and various pieces of Arabian and Islamic knowledge made their way to the West. Astral magic came over from the East, via an Arabic grimoire called *Ghâyat al-Hakîm fi'l-sihr*. The Latin translation of this learned tome became known as *Picatrix* and was circulated among most of the magicians of medieval Europe.

The medieval grimoires were often attributed to ancient wise men such as King Solomon. One such example was the *Clavicula Salomonis*, or Key of Solomon. A German abbot and occultist called Trithemius (1462-1516) claimed to possess a grimoire used by Simon Magus. Simon the Magician is mentioned in the Acts of the Apostles, Chapter 8, in verse 9 onward:

> But there was a certain man, called Simon, which beforetime in the same city used sorcery, and bewitched the people of Samaria, giving out that himself was some great one: To whom they all gave heed, from the least to the greatest, saying, This man is the great power of God.

The medieval church regarded Simon Magus as a devil-worshipper.

In addition to the attacks on witchcraft and black magic, the medieval church developed an obsession with what it regarded as heresy. The Cathars of Languedoc were among their victims. Catharism had dualistic and Gnostic elements and owed many of its beliefs to Paulicians of Armenia and the Bogomils of Bulgaria, with whom the Paulicians merged.

Cathars were also influenced by Manichaean ideas. To the dualistic Cathars, matter was evil and had been created by the evil god, whom they called Rex Mundi, meaning "King of the Earth." They saw Rex Mundi as a god of chaos and brutal quests for power. The good God, whom the Cathars loved and worshipped, was a God of love, peace, and order. Cathars believed that humanity's purpose was to escape from the evil inherent in physical matter, and to strive for a degree of spirituality that would bring them into contact with the spiritual God of Goodness. They could not accept the traditional Catholic Christian idea of Christ as God incarnate because matter (including human bodies) was evil. This meant that the Cathars repudiated the significance of the crucifixion as the key to redemption. They attacked the wealth and power of the Roman Church, and saw it as an example of where the evil Rex Mundi took people!

Unsurprisingly, the Roman Church launched the Albigensian Crusade against the Cathars (who were also known as Albigensians), and despite long and courageous resistance, the Cathars were practically wiped out. One of their most important strongholds was the almost impregnable castle of Montségur, which eventually fell to the Roman Catholic forces. The victory was followed by a brutal mass burning of the erstwhile defenders.

Before the Roman Church succeeded in wiping out the Cathars, there were frequent prosecutions of heretics of various types. Groups of medieval bishops and archbishops were allocated the responsibility of setting up what were known as Episcopal Inquisitions. In the following century, Pope Gregory IX, who reigned from 1227 to 1241, gave the responsibility of running inquisitions to the Dominican Order. A Grand Inquisitor was placed in charge of each Inquisition, and he acted in the name of the Pope and with the Pope's full authority.

The Inquisition did not actually pass sentence on convicted heretics but handed them over to the secular authorities and left it to them to carry out the actual punishments, which frequently included burning at the stake.

The medieval Inquisition openly acknowledged that the gruesome brutality of the punishments handed out to heretics was primarily intended to terrify others so that they would keep well away from heresy.

Persecution of heretics overlapped the persecution of witches, wizards, and magicians, who were regarded by some inquisitors as a singularly dangerous type of heretic – one that believes in Satan and the fallen angels and attempts to invoke their help by means of enchantments.

There were various categories of witch. What was referred to as "the neighbourhood witch" was simply someone who had quarrelled with her neighbours and cursed them. The second category comprised magical witches and sorcerers. These could be healers, herbalists, midwives, seers, or sorcerers. Conflicts and rivalries among them could lead to accusations of witchcraft. The medieval mind also believed in a third category, referred to as "night witches." These were felt to possess very strange paranormal powers and to have the ability to appear to their victims in dreams and visions. They were thought to be demons, to be possessed by demons, or to have the power to control demons and use them for their own selfish and evil purposes.

Terrifying witch-hunts led to the deaths of thousands of innocent and harmless people across Europe in medieval times and later. There was a general fear that vast numbers of witches were in league with the devil, had signed diabolical pacts with him – in blood – and were endeavouring to destroy Christianity.

Hermitage Castle in Scotland is close to the border town of Hawick, and it is from Hermitage Castle that some of the darkest and most brutal stories of demonic pacts and demonic behaviour come. Evil William Soulis, as he was known, owned Hermitage Castle in the thirteenth century. Evil William abducted children and held them in the dungeons of the castle until he was ready to sacrifice them to the devil as part of his black magic pact. William was to indulge in every kind of cruelty and debauchery with Satan's enthusiastic help!

The outraged neighbours, furious and vengeful over what Soulis had done to their children, decided to get together and storm Hermitage Castle. Evil William was captured and boiled alive. Over the years, a number of witnesses have reported psychic phenomena at the castle, including the terrible screams of the doomed children, and the final horrific cries of Evil William's phantom.

One early book dealing with witchcraft was called *Malleus Maleficarum*. In German editions it was called *Der Hexenhammer*. Both titles translate as "The Hammer of the Witches." The author was Heinrich Kramer (1430-1505), who worked as an inquisitor for the Catholic Church. The major theme of Kramer's book was his attempt to refute the argument that witchcraft does not exist, and *Malleus* became the standard textbook and guide for medieval witch-hunters. Kramer argued strongly for the existence of Satan and malignant witches who sought his help. Like so many of his misogynistic contemporaries in prominent positions in the medieval church, Kramer was convinced that human sexuality provided Satan with most of his opportunities to tempt and corrupt, and that women were particularly vulnerable to his advances.

Kramer goes into detail of how witches are recruited by other witches, and how nubile young women are seduced by attractive male demons. He also provides details of spells that witches allegedly use, and gives details of techniques for nullifying them.

The book also goes into detail of how suspected witches could be prosecuted, and how their trials should best be conducted. Interrogation could include torture, and if a woman did not cry during her interrogation that proved her to be a witch! Crimes committed by witches, according to Kramer, included infanticide and cannibalism as well as casting evil spells to harm those whom they saw as their enemies.

The black magician's armoury of spells, amulets, talismans, grimoires, and incantations is varied. The magician may think that she is using strange inner powers to achieve magical purposes. There may be a belief in evil spirits and obedient demons that will do the magician's bidding using their own sinister powers. Mimicry as part of sympathetic magic may be invoked. Weapons such as a magic wand, a mirror, or a crystal ball may be employed. Strange ingredients – both animal and vegetable – can be used in potions: snake's venom, bat's blood, poisonous herbs and fungi all have a place in the medieval black magician's armoury. Other equipment may include parchment with strange words and symbols drawn on it, knots tied in string or the entrails of animals, and strange stones and pebbles, especially those with holes through them. The evil spell aimed at a person is felt to be more effective if there are connections with the intended victim. A black magic doll, or poppet, is thought to focus evil more precisely on the victim if his nail cuttings or hair are incorporated into it. The use of a victim's reflection, his shadow, his footprint, or his name are all thought to give the black magician more power to harm.

It was thought that medieval spells used by witches, wizards, and warlocks to summon a demon or evil spirit to do their bidding had to be cast in a churchyard, a ruin, or a place where a crime had been committed. The black magician leading the ceremony might wear a skullcap, sometimes of metal, and a long black cloak or cape. He would use a wand carved from hazel with the Hebrew Name of God carved into it. A circle is marked on the ground for the protection of the magician: to leave it would make him or her vulnerable to the evil forces being summoned. The name and symbol of the demon being summoned are written outside the protective circle. An animal, or, in extreme cases, a human being, is sacrificed and the blood collected in a copper bowl to attract the demon. At this stage of the ceremony, the participants claim that they can smell the foul odours of hell. The magician leading the ceremony massages magical oil into his body and reads the appropriate spell from his grimoire.

One version of the spell is as follows:

> I [magician's name] summon thee [demon's name] in the Name of the Great and All Powerful God to appear before me now in the shape of a goat. [The magician can choose the form in which he wants the demon to appear.] If you fail to obey my summons, the mighty Archangel Michael will smite you down to the deepest and foulest depths of hell. Come then [demon's name] and do my bidding.

A number of simpler, innocuous spells are far less sinister than the demon-summoning ritual. A medieval spell for obtaining money begins with a witch's bowl or cauldron partly filled with water. The magician then drops a silver coin into it. The spell must be performed by moonlight, as it invokes a moon spirit. The magician gestures above the water with his hands, as if collecting money from the moonlight. The incantation is said while the movements are being made:

> Great and glorious Moon goddess,
> Grant to me the wealth I seek.
> Fill my hands with silver
> And my purse with gold.

After the words have been said three times, the magician retrieves the silver coin from the cauldron and holds it up to the moon. The water from the cauldron is then poured out onto a patch of moonlit earth to complete the spell.

An interesting medieval spell for recovering lost objects has to be performed in bright sunlight at midday. Candles are lit as the spell begins: thirteen, seven, or three are recommended. Lavender is burned in a copper dish in the centre of the candles, and the magician recites:

> Spirits of wisdom and knowledge, spirits of Earth and water,
> Spirits of air and sky above, you see all things.
> Lead me to that which is lost that it may be safely recovered.

Once the candles had burned down to nothing, and the lavender had been reduced to ashes, the magician would be led to the lost objects.

It was also important to the medieval magician to be able to break the power of a spell that had been cast by a rival magician or an evil enemy. One technique for breaking the power of someone else's malevolent spell was to place a candle in a bowl of water and to top up the water very close to, but not quite touching, the wick. The magician intent on breaking the spell meditates and focuses his mind on the candle and mentally, symbolically, imagines that the power of the spell that is to be broken is actually *in* the candle. The candle flame symbolizes the unwelcome spell. The magician then lights the wick. As the flame burns down to the surface of the water, the wick gets wet and the candle goes out – the spell is destroyed along with the extinguished flame.

Once an evil spell has been broken, the witch or wizard may feel that a purification spell would be a welcome addition, and would complete the process. Three candles are normally used for disposing of negative magical energy. One is green, symbolizing mental and physical healing.

The second is red and represents positive strength and energy. The third is white and symbolizes goodness and virtue. Each candle is lit in turn, the white one first.

The magician then intones: "Goddess of the Earth and Queen of Nature, rulers of fire, water and air, take from us all that is negative and evil. Fill us with goodness and positive energy."

The red candle is lit next, and he continues: "Mother goddess of the Earth and Queen of Nature, rulers of fire, water and air, fill us with all that is good and grant us the will to love and help others and the positive energy to turn our good will into good actions."

Finally, the green candle is lit: "Mother goddess and healer of the Earth, Queen and sustainer of Nature, rulers of fire, water and air, fill us with healing and health of mind, body and spirit."

The activities of the medieval witches and wizards, their pacts with the devil and his demons, their familiar spirits, spells, and curses, their array of magical equipment, and the grimoires in which their forbidden knowledge was recorded all helped to lay a foundation for Satanism — or, at least, that sub-section of it which was inseparable from black magic and witchcraft.

Renaissance Satanism

The Renaissance brought with it many deep theological and philosophical problems, as well as magnificent advances in art and science. As people began to escape from the tyranny of orthodox religious dogma, one great question hovered over them: the question at the heart of theodicy.

The word *theodicy* is derived from the Greek *theos*, meaning "God," and *dike*, meaning "justice." The German philosopher Gottfried Leibniz (1646-1716) coined the term in his book entitled *Theodicy Essays on the Goodness of God, the Freedom of Man, and the Origin of Evil*. Leibniz set out to try to show that all the evil and suffering in the world does not disprove the existence of a benign God. Leibniz argued that despite the evil and suffering that were all too evident, "the world was the best of all possible worlds." He was actually writing in reply to Pierre Bayle (1647-1706), who had argued that evil and suffering proved that God could not be both good and omnipotent. Among several useful dictionary definitions of theodicy, one of the best is to be found in the *American Heritage Dictionary of the English Language*, Fourth Edition: "Theodicy is a vindication of God's goodness and justice in the face of the existence of evil."

Theodicy came to the fore during the Renaissance, the French term for rebirth, referred to in Italy as the Rinascimento. It began in Florence and spread to the rest of Europe, and brought with it such polymaths as Leonardo da Vinci (1452-1519) and Michelangelo di Lodovico Buonarroti Simoni (1475-1564). Their fields included painting, poetry, sculpture, architecture, medicine, engineering, and science. These two were among the greatest and best-known of the supremely gifted Renaissance men, but they were by no means alone.

One partial answer to the problems that theodicy presented to the liberated thinking of Renaissance intellectuals was the possible existence of Satanism, black magic, wizards, witches, sorcerers, and devil-worshippers. God's undoubted goodness and infinite power were thought to be opposed by the forces of evil, and by the sinister, iniquitous magic that was one of their weapons.

There was also the question of free will that the Renaissance mind considered so important. It was argued that God in his goodness wanted human liberty. Freedom was, therefore, a vital gift to human beings but also potentially a very dangerous one. People with freedom of choice could, and often did, select evil rather than virtue.

Another bulwark of theodicy was consistency. It was felt that God's creation was a consistent creation. Red could not be blue on randomized Tuesdays and purple on unpredictable Thursdays. Hot could not be cold at a whim and north could not be south. It was argued that the nature and behaviour of all the matter and energy in the universe that a benign God had created had to be *consistent*, otherwise humanity could never learn how the environment functioned. Researchers, inventors, and medical scientists could only find ways to improve life if the things they were studying remained steadfast.

Given the premise of human free will, together with the angelic free will that had allowed Lucifer to rebel in the first place, and the universally consistent behaviour of matter and energy in the universe, then theodicy — although still far from perfect and definitive — at least had a fighting chance of surviving in the intellectual jungle of philosophy and theology.

Despite all the Renaissance advances, Heinrich Kramer's *Malleus Maleficarum* continued to be widely read and followed. The invention and development in Europe of printing with movable type dates from the middle of the fifteenth century, and had a good deal to do with the spread of *Malleus Maleficarum*. Kramer seems to have done everything in his power to associate reputable academics and theologians with his work, and all the printed editions after 1519 bore the name of Jacob Sprenger (1436-94) as the co-author. This co-authorship remains controversial.

Sprenger was a Swiss priest, born near Basel. He was a Dominican and Dean of the Faculty of Theology at Cologne University. Pope Innocent VIII appointed him and Kramer as inquisitors in Germany.

Innocent VIII was born Giovanni Battista Cybo in 1432 and was pope from 1484 until his death in 1492. From the year that he attained the Papacy, Innocent VIII was obsessed by his fears of witchcraft, devil-worship, and black magic. He issued a Papal Bull for the benefit of Kramer and Sprenger, entitled *Summis Desiderantes* – "Desiring with extreme ardour" – that laid down drastic measures against witches, wizards, and magicians.

Bad weather, crop failure, increasing crime, and starvation were all blamed on witches and wizards and their demonic masters. Innocent's Papal Bull stated:

> It has recently come to our ears, not without great pain to us, that in some parts of upper Germany: Mainz, Koin, Trier, Salzburg, and Bremen, many persons of both sexes, heedless of their own salvation and forsaking the catholic faith, give themselves over to devils male and female, and by their incantations, charms, and conjurings, and by other abominable superstitions and sortileges, offences, crimes, and misdeeds, ruin and cause to perish the offspring of women, the foal of animals, the products of the earth, the grapes of vines, and the fruits of trees, as well as men and women, cattle and flocks and herds and animals of every kind, vineyards also and orchards, meadows, pastures, harvests, grains and other fruits of the earth; that they afflict and torture with dire pains and anguish, both internal and external, these men, women, cattle, flocks, herds, and animals, and hinder men from begetting.

An example of the kind of persecution that went on in Germany can be seen in the torture dungeons of Wewelsburg Castle.

Unfortunately for the many innocent victims of the Inquisition, Pope Paul II had declared witchcraft to be *crimen exceptum* – a crime or offence that is "outside" normal law, an "exception" to the regulations regarding the use of torture. This meant that all the legal limits relating to the application of torture were removed in cases where the accused was suspected of witchcraft, devil-worship, or black magic. Torture was used primarily to force the accused to confess to their own crimes and then to name their accomplices in the dark arts. Being able to confiscate the property of a condemned witch or wizard was a massive inducement to

Wewelsburg Castle in Germany. Witches were tortured in the dungeons here during the Inquisition.

Co-author Lionel in the dungeons of Wewelsburg Castle with some of the instruments of torture used on women accused of witchcraft.

the inquisitors and a clear encouragement to any avaricious informants who coveted their neighbours' land and other property.

Depriving the accused of sleep for hour after hour was often enough to extort a confession. Other victims of the Inquisition would be taken to watch fellow victims being tortured or burned at the stake as an inducement to confess before the same horrors were applied to them.

Actual methods of torture included the scold's bridle, an iron cage with a spiked mouthpiece that pierced the victim's tongue, and the ducking stool and trial by water: if the victim sank and drowned, she was innocent; if she floated or swam, she was guilty!

Part of the belief in witches was that there was a spot on their bodies, known as the "devil's mark," which was impervious to pain. Countless innocent victims were pricked and prodded so many times that they lost sensitivity. The inquisitors then declared triumphantly that the telltale devil's mark had been found, and the victim was undoubtedly a witch or wizard.

Torture with red-hot pincers was another favourite with the inquisitors, as was forcing the victim to sit naked on a red-hot iron stool. The so-called witch's chair was another hideous instrument of torture used by the Inquisition – this had hundreds of sharp spikes all over it to pierce the victim's naked body. *Gresillons* crushed fingers and toes until a confession was forthcoming, and the *brodequins* were used to crush the victims' leg bones. The *echelle* was similar to the rack, and victims would sometimes be stretched so traumatically that limbs were not only dislocated but actually torn off the body. Tying the accused's arms behind the back and then hauling the victim off the ground would dislocate or fracture the arms. They were raised and dropped repeatedly.

Not content with appointing the repugnant Kramer and Sprenger as inquisitors in Germany, Innocent VIII confirmed the appointment of the loathsome Tomás de Torquemada (1420-98) as Inquisitor-General of Spain.

There is some controversy over the actual number involved but *thousands* of innocent victims were tortured to the point of confession and then burned at the stake under his jurisdiction. Torquemada was so hated and feared that he was accompanied by hundreds of bodyguards. After his death, his tomb was raided and his bones were dragged out and burned.

In East Anglia (in England), the equally unpleasant Matthew Hopkins (1620–47) styled himself "The Witchfinder General," and for two brutal years, in the company of fellow witch-finder John Stearne, tortured and executed dozens of innocent victims. Hopkins's book, *The Discovery of Witches*, was published in 1647 – the same year that he died. He gives an account in this volume of how his interest in witch-hunting had begun when he had overheard a group of women in Manningtree discussing the ways in which they had made pacts with the devil.

There are two conflicting accounts of his death. The first suggests that he died of natural causes, aged only 27 or 28, possibly from tuberculosis. The second, more probable, account suggests that a party of angry villagers from the Manningtree area formed a lynch mob and hanged him in retaliation for their innocent friends and neighbours whom his witch-hunting had condemned. Like their continental counterparts, Hopkins and Stearne used "pricking" and so-called "swimming" or water-testing to establish whether the hapless victim was a witch or wizard. Stearne apparently used a series of piercing devices with retractable spikes that retreated secretly into the handle when pressed against the victim's skin so that it *looked as if* the victim was being stabbed and apparently feeling no pain. Suppliers of theatrical props still provide these devices today for use in detective plays in which a murder victim is realistically "stabbed" on stage.

Just as the confiscation of a heretic's land and property were a great inducement to the inquisitors, so the fees that Hopkins and Stearne charged for their witch-finding services provided them with powerful motivation. The town of Stowmarket, in Suffolk, paid the two witch-finders £23 for their work at a time when an average wage was only a few pence a week!

The infamous cruelty of inquisitors and witch-finders like Kramer, Sprenger, Hopkins, and Stearne paradoxically contributed to the growth of Satanism in the Renaissance and the period that followed it. It is ironic that their ostensible attempts to reduce and destroy heresy, witchcraft, devil-worship, and black magic focused public attention on the very things that they claimed they were trying to eliminate. It hardly needs the psychological insight of Freud and Jung to suspect that inquisitors and witch-finders alike were motivated by their sadistic perversions rather than by any genuine desire to prevent witches and wizards from doing their black magical work with the help of devils and demons.

The presence of a genuinely heroic and unflinchingly determined demon-hunter might have saved many lives in the Auvergne and South Dordogne areas of France in the eighteenth century, when something inexplicable and damnably dangerous was on the rampage there for three or four years. Known as *La Bête du Gévaudon*, a werewolf-like beast reportedly stalked the area, allegedly killing scores of people during its reign of terror.

King Louis XV (1710-74) was reigning over a turbulent and discontented realm during the time of the ravages of *La Bête*, and the horrific accounts added so much to the social tension and stress that Louis himself took a personal interest in the phenomenon. He paid for professional hunters to go after *La Bête*, but although one or two large wolves were tracked down and killed, the mystery was never definitively solved.

Surviving eyewitnesses described the beast as far larger than a normal wolf and possessing a formidable mouth equipped with large fangs. Many also commented on the abnormally long and bushy tail. The beast was also said to give off a foul odour and its thick fur was described as brownish-red in colour.

Victims who had succumbed to the monster were found with their throats torn open. One of the earliest reports came from a farm girl whose life was saved when the bulls on the farm where she worked charged at *La Bête* and drove it away from her. Fourteen-year-old Jeanne Boulet, from the village of Les Hubacs near Langogne, was not so fortunate: *La Bête* attacked her on June 30, 1764, and she became its first officially recorded victim.

One somewhat controversial account involved a huntsman named Jean Chastel, who allegedly ran *La Bête* to ground on June 19, 1767, and shot it with a silver bullet.

Near the town of Cornholme, in Lancashire, England, can be found the mysterious Bearnshaw Tower. The location has long been associated with the legendary shape-shifting Lady Sybil. The tower collapsed in the middle of the nineteenth century after treasure hunters dug under it to find a chest rumoured to be filled with gold. No treasure was ever found.

Satanism and Demonology

Witches as shape-shifters transform into does.

Lady Sybil was a wild, free spirit who allegedly made a pact with the devil so that she could become a cat, a doe, or a hare in order to freely roam the crags around Bearnshaw Tower.

In the early 1600s, Lord William Towneley of nearby Hapton Hall was deeply in love with Sybil, and called on the help of an enchantress, Mother Helston, to help him catch the lovely Sybil so that he could propose to her. With the aid of a magic rope provided by Mother Helston, William took the graceful doe back to Hapton Hall, where she turned back into the beautiful Sybil. She promised to give up sorcery, renege on her pact with Satan, and become a loving wife to Lord William.

There are two endings to the story. In the first, she and William enjoyed many happy years together. In the second, she reverted to her magical shape-shifting and died in 1633. The heart-broken William buried her on the crag where she had loved to roam as a doe.

Death by witchcraft in a more subtle form is recorded in the Church of St. Mary the Virgin in Bottesford, England. Francis Manners, the Sixth

Earl of Rutland, is entombed there, the vault depicting and image of the earl, his two wives, and his two young sons, each of whom holds a skull. There is an inscription on the tomb that includes these words: IN 1608 HE MARRIED YE LADY CECILIA HUNGERFORD, DAUGHTER TO YE HONORABLE KNIGHT SIR JOHN TUFTON, BY WHOM HE HAD TWO SONS, BOTH OF WHICH DIED IN THEIR INFANCY BY WICKED PRACTISES AND SORCERYE.

In addition to the skull, the younger son, Francis, holds a flower. This is particularly interesting. The three witches who were accused of causing the boys' deaths had the surname *Flower*. All of them worked in Belvoir Castle, the home of the Sixth Earl. Joan, the mother, worked as a general cleaner: her daughters, Philippa and Margaret, looked after poultry and did the laundry. It seems that their reputations were not good, and Margaret was sacked.

Soon afterward, Henry, the Earl's elder son, was stricken with a mysterious illness and died. The Flower family were accused of killing the boy with witchcraft. Arrested and brought in front of the local magistrates, the accused women were sent on to Lincoln to be dealt with. Joan, however, died on the way. She had attempted to prove her innocence by eating bread, which was supposed to be impossible for witches because of its association with the Holy Sacrament. Witnesses to her death reported that she had choked and died on the bread — thus proving she was a witch!

The two Flower girls confessed (almost certainly after being tortured). They said that they had cast death spells on both boys and their elder half-sister Katherine, along with a further spell to prevent the Countess Cecilia from having any more children. Part of their evil magic had consisted of stealing a glove belonging to Henry, stroking the cat (their familiar) with it, and then dipping it in hot water and stabbing it with scissors. A similar spell was cast with a glove stolen from Francis. Both women were found guilty and hanged on March 12, 1618.

In view of the evil spells cast by the Flower family, the horrendous tortures inflicted by the inquisitors, and the victims killed by whatever sort of monster *La Bête du Gévaudon* really was, it seems a little strange that witchcraft, wizardry, black magic, and demonology could, a century later, become the subject of bizarre humour via the antics of the so-called Hellfire Club of Medmenham Abbey and the convoluted West Wycombe Caves in Buckinghamshire, England.

Sir Francis Dashwood (1708–81) of Hellfire Club fame was a former postmaster general and Chancellor of the Exchequer (roles that most political historians agree he did not perform particularly well!) As far as popular thinking about his Hellfire Club went, Francis and the other members were supposedly merely rakes, heavy drinkers, and participants in uninhibited sexual orgies, the girls involved being attractive young prostitutes brought up from London especially for the occasion, dressed as nuns.

However, there are a number of serious historians and researchers of devil-worship and the paranormal who think that the West Wycombe Hellfire Club might have been a clever double-bluff. By *pretending* to be light-hearted mockers of devil-worship and the black arts in general, interested only in having rakish fun with drink and girls, the Hellfire Club members *could* have camouflaged the fact that they actually had secret inner caves deep within the West Wycombe labyrinth.

In these inner sanctums, strange and solemn demonic rituals and liturgies might have taken place in deadly earnest, and some of the girls could have been involved in serious sexual magic rather than simply entertaining their clients.

If Dashwood and an inner group of his select colleagues were party to the hidden secrets of the *real* devil-worship going on behind the frivolous facade of the Hellfire Club, might that not have been fruitful territory for the growth of Satanism in his era? It needs to be remembered that Dashwood was allegedly initiated into a cult of devil-worshippers while he was touring Europe as a young man. From that tour, he brought back several grimoires, and he later put numerous candid statues, murals, and frescoes into his luxurious home.

Royston Cave, which has some strange factors in common with the West Wycombe Caves, is believed to date back to the thirteenth century, but could be much older. The cave, which is in Melbourn Street in the town of Royston, about sixty-five kilometres from London, is a man-made cave shaped roughly like an underground beehive. There are wall carvings within the structure that depict biblical scenes such as the crucifixion as well as figures representing the holy family, and some saints, including Christopher, Katherine, and Laurence. There are also some mysterious pagan symbols on the walls and markings that might relate to spells and magical or alchemical formulae.

Several historians and researchers have concluded that the cave is associated with the Templars, and experts in Freemasonry have seen Masonic symbols among the Royston wall carvings. King James I was known to have had Masonic connections, and in his day there was a royal hunting lodge at Royston. Even more mysterious theories suggest that the cave is situated, significantly, at an intersection of two important ley lines — alignments of ancient sites or holy places, such as stone circles, standing stones, cairns, and churches, thought to have spiritual power. Other experts regard it as a possible hermitage or even an oubliette-style prison — a secret dungeon with its only access through a trap door. Like the West Wycombe cave labyrinth, Royston Cave could have served as a secret meeting place for black magicians, witches, wizards, and Satanists.

The infamous Black Pullet Grimoire, known as *La Poule Noire*, almost certainly featured among the grimoires in Dashwood's collection. Considering the French use of *poule* for prostitute, the title of the

Very strange carvings inside mysterious Royston Cave.

grimoire would have had extra appeal for Dashwood. In the book there are numerous spells for producing charms, amulets, and talismans, and the most important one of all is the Black Pullet spell which enables the black magician to produce (or transform from an ordinary pullet) a black hen that can lay golden eggs. It would have been obvious to the sophisticated Dashwood that an attractive young prostitute working with rich clients laid the metaphorical golden eggs for her pimp. The notorious Black Pullet Spell may then have been regarded simply as a means of overcoming a new girl's resistance and getting her to accept her work as a prostitute.

The story behind the Black Pullet Grimoire can be traced back to a young French officer fighting in Napoleon's army in the Valley of the Kings in Egypt. One French detachment was attacked by Bedouins and overwhelmed, but the young officer, left for dead, miraculously survived. A mysterious old Turkish magician emerged from one of the pyramids, helped the Frenchman back into a secret chamber within the pyramid, then slowly nursed him back to health. During this period, the old magician shared with the Frenchman some ancient magical secrets that allegedly escaped from what the old man referred to as "the burning of Ptolemy's library." On his return to France at the end of hostilities, the French officer wrote down what he had learned, and the grimoire appeared under an alternative title – *The Treasure of the Old Man of the Pyramids*.

The design has to be embroidered on black silk or black satin if it is to be effective, according to the Black Pullet Grimoire. Magic words have to be said when the amulet is used. The words are listed as *nudes surudis maniner*. If the amulet works according to the account in the grimoire, a demon (genie or jinn) should then appear. More magic words are then needed: *Sader prostas solaster*. The demon will then present the magician with an attractive sex partner. The magician may keep the partner until boredom detracts from their relationship, whereupon the magician recites the words *mammes laher*. The demon, or jinn, then removes the sex partner, who is no longer exciting enough ... and returns with a fresh one! This spell would have had great appeal for members of Dashwood's Hellfire Club.

A man who was more than qualified for membership in the worst Hellfire Club was the notorious Colonel Thomas Sydney, who lived at Ranworth Old Hall in Norfolk toward the close of the eighteenth century.

The strange design on an amulet from the Black Pullet Grimoire.

Generally described as a drunken bully and braggart, he once challenged a neighbour to a race — then shot the man's horse from under him when he looked as if he was going to win. The horse reared in agony and threw his rider, then came down on top of him, with fatal results. Colonel Sydney showed not an iota of regret or remorse.

The following New Year's Eve, the Annual Hunt Banquet was taking place at Sydney's luxurious home. Drinks were flowing freely, and the Colonel was singing and shouting loudly amid the general revelry when the door opened with a sudden crash.

Descriptions of the sinister figure in the doorway varied from one witness to another, but there were several who swore it was the devil himself. Whoever or whatever the mysterious stranger was, he possessed immense strength; Colonel Sydney was no weakling, and he fought desperately as the stranger picked him up effortlessly, threw him over his shoulder, and leaped onto a great black horse waiting outside.

Some of the bravest guests watched as the rider galloped away across Ranworth Broad. Colonel Sydney was never seen again. The consensus was that the devil had taken him to hell.

Very different from the Black Pullet Grimoire — apart from the obvious similarity of names — is the curious account of the black cockerel of the Punchbowl Inn at Lanreath in Cornwall, England. There's a lot of history attached to the Punchbowl Inn, which dates back to the thirteenth century. The episode of the black cockerel dates back to the same period as Colonel Sydney and Dashwood's Hellfire Club at West Wycombe.

The elderly vicar of Lanreath had a young and beautiful wife, and the new curate fell madly in love with her. One evening, all three were having dinner at the vicarage, and the elderly vicar went down the rather dangerous cellar steps to get some more wine. Officially, he tripped and fell, and his death was formally recorded as "accidental," but tongues wagged in the village when the romance between the curate and the lovely young widow became widely known. Almost immediately after the vicar's death, a vicious and aggressive wild black cockerel started attacking people, and some superstitious villagers believed it to be the vengeful spirit of the late vicar. One day it flew wildly into the kitchen of the Punchbowl Inn and right inside an open clome oven. A quick-witted young cook slammed the oven door on it, then ran to tell the landlord. Believing that the best thing to do was to dispose of the dangerous rooster before a child or someone frail or elderly was injured by it, the landlord had the oven door cemented over. Centuries later, the black cockerel's remains are still inside the oven in the Punchbowl's kitchen.

The mysterious spells and instructions for making amulets and talismans found in the various grimoires — the notorious Black Pullet collection and some less powerful ones — may have owed their persistent attraction to an interesting connection between *belief* and *outcome*. If charms and talismans never had the slightest effect, the public would soon grow tired of them, and even the most committed of their creators would cease to believe that they worked.

Dr. Lysann Damisch, of the University of Cologne, and her academic team have recently conducted some very interesting research into the

Clome oven in the Punchbowl Inn, containing the Black Cockerel.

effectiveness of charms such as a rabbit's foot, a four-leafed clover, wearing certain colours, or even something as simple as crossing one's fingers. A number of volunteers who declared their use of lucky charms and their faith in them took part in the Cologne experiments. Half of the volunteers handed their charms to the academic researchers prior to taking a simple memory test as a performance indicator. The other half retained their lucky charms during the test. The results showed that the volunteers who had retained their lucky charms performed better than those who had temporarily surrendered theirs to the university researchers. Several other experiments were undertaken, all of which indicated that wishing someone good luck or allowing them to keep their talisman definitely affected performance.

A magician would argue that there was some real mysterious and invisible magical power in the charm that could somehow influence the environment, or improve the charm-owner's performance. Psychologists might prefer to argue that it was the subject's *belief* in the charm that altered his or her mental state in such a way that performance was improved. When there is a successful outcome within a given environment and within a certain set of circumstances, either something has affected the environment in the subject's favour — or the subject's performance has been improved. The decision has to be made as to the source of that improvement: has the power of the charm improved the performance, or has the subject's *belief* in the power of the charm improved the performance?

The power of thought and the influence of belief systems on human behaviour are also clearly revealed in Wicca, one of the latest developments of earlier witchcraft. Its adherents, known as Wiccans, often refer to it as witchcraft, or simply "the craft," and it is generally regarded as a form of neo-paganism. There are arguments about when it came into being in its modified contemporary form; some suggest the early twentieth century, or as late as the 1950s, when retired British civil servant Gerald Gardner put a great deal of thought and effort into it. Many aspects of it, however, are genuinely ancient, and other significant parts of its inner core can be traced back at least to Renaissance times.

Philosophers and theologians regard it as a typically duotheistic religious faith. Many Wiccans worship a god and goddess who are sometimes referred to as the horned god and the triple goddess. The issue is complicated by the view of some Wiccans that these two are really aspects of one great pantheistic god. Other Wiccans are polytheistic, and believe that their two central deities can also reveal themselves in other divine forms. There are monotheistic Wiccans; others are atheists. Their laws, rules, and ethical guidelines are very free and liberal, but with the general proviso that one person's freedom ends where it restricts someone else's freedom — and that no conduct is acceptable if it brings harm to anyone. This system of morality is sometimes called the Wiccan Rede. Wiccan rituals are often called Sabbats, and Wiccans normally celebrate eight each year.

Just as there are different denominations within the great Abrahamic religions — Judaism, Islam, and Christianity — so there are clearly demarcated denominations within Wicca. Some follow Gardner's ideas; others belong to Alexandrian Wicca. Cochrane's Craft and the Dianic tradition are also denominations of Wicca.

Some Wiccan theologians would argue that the whole of the cosmos is a living being, and that each of its parts is also a living being. This could go all the way down to the microcosm. A parallel might, perhaps, be suggested by a swarm of bees or a colony of ants: individual members acting as a whole.

The idea of a god and goddess in Wicca can be understood as a parallel concept to the idea of yin and yang in Taoism. For some Wiccans, the goddess is either the earth mother or the moon, while the god is associated with the sun. Gerald Gardner saw them not so much as persons but as personifications of what he regarded as cosmic power.

While the Wiccan concept of their horned god associates him with nature, sexuality, the wilderness, and the life cycle, they certainly do not regard him as evil. Some Wiccans, however, call him Atho, Cernunnos, Pan, Karnayna, and even the devil, Satan, or Lucifer. Wiccans also think of one aspect of their god as the green man, especially when they are associating him with nature. In this guise he also becomes the oak king and the holly king, the ruler of summer and winter.

The goddess, thought of as the *triple* goddess by Wiccans, embodies virginity, fertility, and wisdom: she is a maiden, a mother, and a wise old woman to whom younger people turn for counsel. For some Wiccans the goddess is more powerful and more important than their male god: he takes on the dual role of her lover and her child.

In yet other branches of Wicca there is another deity, a Supreme Being who transcends both the god and goddess. Interestingly, both Gerald Gardner and the renowned Egyptologist Margaret Murray had similar theories about the horned god being at the centre of worship for European witch-cults during the persecution of the witches by the inquisitors. The horned god and his goddess consort were in their view a continuation of the old British religion that had preceded the arrival of Christianity.

Contemporary Satanism

What may be termed contemporary Satanism has developed from earlier forms of proto-Satanism over many millennia, and has to be studied in the light of those historical developments. The many very different roots of contemporary Satanism also need to be examined individually to ascertain what each has contributed to the contemporary satanic scene.

Satanism needs to be studied as a particularly eclectic belief system. It can be seen from one angle to be an antithesis of Christianity as expressed by various Christian churches, cults, and sects over the last two thousand years. Viewed in this way, Satanism can be thought of as merely a parasite living on Christianity, or as a perversion of Christianity. Viewed from a wider perspective, however, Satanism can trace some of its older roots back to various forms of paganism, nature religions, fertility cults, animism, and polytheism.

At the opposite extremes of contemporary Satanism are atheistic Satanism — which sounds like a contradiction in terms — and theistic Satanism, in which Lucifer, the devil, or Satan is seen as a divine or semi-divine being, a paranormal entity who is worshipped, revered, and obeyed accordingly.

Some groups of contemporary Satanists are strongly influenced by the contents of grimoires and other books of spells, enchantments and magical liturgies, and rituals, and they base their particular belief systems on what they read there.

Some versions of modern Satanism are thought to have grown out of the conflict between natural, innate desires — impulses which are instinctive within human nature — and what society regards as morally and ethically acceptable behaviour. If strong religious elements within some traditional societies criticize natural behaviour as being "devilish" or "evil," then Satanism becomes the refuge of those who

The devil in theistic Satanism as a paranormal entity.

wish to pursue their natural desires rather than to fight against them and suppress them.

The study of atheistic Satanism begins with the underlying idea that Satan does not exist in any real, personal sense. He is not regarded as an entity of any kind. Atheistic Satanists use the word *Satan* as a convenient personification of their desire for unrestricted, uninhibited self-expression. If in their minds he did exist, he would be their god of pleasure, ambition, and selfish power. Believing as they do that the quest for power and pleasure is the central part of life, they simply use the *concept* of Satanism as a convenient way of summing up their beliefs. It is the mental magnifying glass through which they examine life to find ways of increasing their pleasure from food, drink, and extreme forms of eroticism.

The main philosophical and theological problem for these atheistic Satanists is that they have nothing beyond their own human powers to which to appeal for help when their personal resources prove inadequate. In denying the existence of a benign, just, moral, and ethical God who opposes their wrongdoing, and also in denying the existence of Lucifer or Satan as the focal point of their opposition to that good and supreme God, they cut themselves off from any real or imagined power source beyond themselves.

Their atheism allows them to feel that they can behave as they wish with complete impunity; but this absence of any fear of reprisal carries with it the inevitable corollary that there is no hope of help either. Logically, no external source of punishment means that there is no external source of reward!

It is possible that some atheistic Satanists may cherish a belief in the power of magic, even if they do not regard a personal Satan as the source of magical power, witchcraft, and wizardry. While denying the existence of a personal Satan, they may consider that magic, like science, can work *independently* of the existence of paranormal beings of any type. Just as burning carbon produces carbon dioxide in the laboratory because it is simply in the nature of those chemical elements to combine in that way, perhaps chanting "Abracadabra" and mixing poisoned entrails with herbs and spices in a cauldron by moonlight will produce some other objective and repeatable result.

Atheistic Satanists are, therefore, quite capable of believing in magic — a parallel "science" for them, akin to physics and chemistry — as something that is simply part of the universe, something that "just happens" because things in the universe "are the way that they are."

There is also the seriously underrated power of thought and the mysterious energy within the human mind. Alexandra David-Néel (1868-1969), the deeply spiritual thinker, fearless traveller, prolific writer, and adventuress seems to have succeeded in creating a *tulpa* (a thought-form that appeared as a monk) during her time in Tibet.

Just as a dramatist can create a character in a play, so, it is argued, a sufficiently powerful imagination can create a *tulpa* that actually becomes visible and audible to other witnesses. Does the power of magic depend not upon an input from a personalized devil, but upon the power in the mind of the magician? If Alexandra David-Néel could create a *tulpa*, can an enchanter create some desired result — an attractive and enthusiastic sex partner, longevity, wealth, healing, strength, fame — simply by the power within the enchanter's mind? There is then no need to imagine Satan as a personal entity, nor to imagine that the ingredients in the magical cauldron actually *do* anything other than act as a useful focal point for the hidden powers inside the magician's head.

Theistic Satanism is diametrically opposite to atheistic Satanism. Theistic Satanism is centred on the belief that Satan, Lucifer, Ahriman — the devil by whatever name his adherents call him — is a real paranormal entity with an objective existence. In dualistic forms of Satanism, he is seen as having power equal to that of the good God. In other forms of theistic Satanism his power is less than that of God, but he is nevertheless formidable.

If, as theistic Satanists believe, the devil is an intelligent, self-aware entity, the primary theological and philosophical questions are: What does he want? What motivates him? What are his purposes?

If ideas similar to those of Greco-Roman, Norse, or Egyptian polytheism are introduced, then the gods — including Satan — are merely human beings transformed into immortal entities with massive superhuman powers. Their emotions and motivations remain at a recognizably human level. God A has wronged god B: he has slept with the wrong goddess; he has stolen some divine artifact of immense power; he has harmed someone under the other god's protection. He has, in fact, spoken some word or performed some act that would have angered the other party *if both had been ordinary human beings.*

Theistic Satanism then becomes explicable in terms of Lucifer's ambition to be the supreme god and his rebellion against Yahweh. All Satan's motivations then become clear. He wants to do everything that may damage Yahweh and his worshippers. Satan wants chaos in place of order, hatred in place of love, lies instead of truth, pain instead of pleasure, death instead of life, and selfish ambition instead of altruistic helpfulness to others.

This simplistic, confrontational view is modified by other theistic Satanists who do *not* regard their hero as evil: far from it. For them he is a freedom fighter, the prince of anarchists, a bold revolutionary, a warrior of infinite courage who *dares* to challenge the heavy, repressive, controlling rules and regulations associated by most religions with their Supreme God of goodness, order, justice, ethics, and morality. These groups of theistic Satanists are the ones who most loudly proclaim: "Do as you please is the whole of the law." They regard Satan as their leader in their personal battles against conformity, obedience, poverty, and chastity. For them, Satan is not evil: he is the champion of the new world order for which they are fighting. He is the leader who will give them power, prestige, fame, wealth, and sexual freedom: everything they long for.

But the persistent questions remain unanswered: What does he get out of it? If he is their heroic freedom fighter, anarchist prince, and revolutionary leader, what's in it for him? Is he so good and unselfish that he wants nothing more than the freedom, success, and happiness of his people? Does he glory in their worship? Does he simply want their allegiance?

The same question asked of the Supreme God of Love is answerable. If, as his worshippers believe, God truly is love personified, if love is God's real nature, then love finds ultimate delight in loving others, in extending outward creatively and sustainably, and genuinely finding an exquisite purpose in giving happiness to all that it creates and sustains. This is comprehensible even to limited human thought and emotion. For one human being to be truly in love with another is for them to desire the other person's happiness above all else, and to do everything possible to bring about that happiness.

If it is the essential nature of a loving being to want to give happiness, what is the essential nature of the opponent of such a loving being? That a loving nature seeks to give happiness seems self-evident. The motivation of any other type of being is less clear. Does an evil being *enjoy* hurting others, destroying things, causing suffering? It may, but that does not explain *why* it does?

Love's motives are clear because of the nature of love. Evil's motives are curiously unclear and ambiguous. That evil should seek to do harm is not self-evident because evil cannot enjoy doing harm in the way that love enjoys doing good. What pleasure or benefit can personified evil derive from causing harm? There is a vacuum where the answer should be.

A side issue that may, perhaps, shed a little light on the problem is the error of judgment that human evil makes when it performs an evil act in the mistaken belief that it will bring happiness. The thief steals to become rich; the murderer strikes in order to gain some advantage of power or money as a result of the victim's death; the drug addict injects more of the drug in the hope of transitory elation; the traitor betrays comrades and country ... the list is endless. The *motive* is to obtain benefits and advantages of some sort: the *outcome* is usually dissatisfaction, accompanied by feelings of guilt, misery, and anxiety, often followed by apprehension and punishment. So the motivation for evil actions is to obtain something the perpetrator wants, not to do evil just for the sake of doing evil.

The fanatical, obsessive politician or religious zealot often believes that his cause is a supremely good, right, and important one. They believe that the end justifies the means. Like the Spanish inquisitors and the so-called witch-finders, they commit grotesquely horrible and evil acts, not with the intention to do evil, but to forward a cause they believe is supremely *good*.

In a weirdly paradoxical way, then, it may be possible to argue that evil has no self-evident motivation at all: evil is perhaps best understood as the perversion or distortion of good. Is it simply the *absence* of goodness? Is darkness a thing in its own right, or is it merely the absence of light? Is coldness a thing in its own right, or is it merely the absence of heat? If that is the case, then what is the *motivation* of Lucifer in theistic Satanism?

If evil is seen as the mere absence of goodness, is it possible for abstract evil, or for an evil entity such as Satan, Lucifer, or one of the subordinate devils or demons, to enter or possess a human being or other life form? There are Satanists who seem to experience — or to claim that they have experienced — such possession. There are witnesses and psychic investigators who report having seen people or animals behaving in a manner that suggests that they are under the control of some evil force, or some evil being. How does this fit in with any analysis of Satanism that sees evil as an absence of goodness? Theistic Satanism can find room for it, atheistic Satanism cannot.

Does the curious case of Joanna Southcott shed any light on the problem of possession or of actual contact with Satan as an important aspect of theistic Satanism?

Joanna Southcott was born in Taleford Farm, in Devonshire, England, on April 26, 1750. Her father was William Southcott, a tenant farmer, and her mother was his second wife, Hannah (née Godfrey). His first wife had died in childbirth and her son, also named William, was brought up by Hannah alongside her own six children.

One of Joanna's earliest experiences of what she believed at the time to be contact with Satan occurred when she was sent at night to a cider shed some considerable distance from the home. There were strange noises coming from the shed and Joanna was convinced that either Satan himself or one of his evil spirits was watching her and following her.

Another early part of Joanna's life was spent at the Church of St. Michael in nearby Gittisham, where she was taught to read and write. The vicar there was the Reverend William Putt, who almost invariably preached about the devil's power and his ability to tempt people to sin so that they would be condemned. On one occasion, her mind full to overflowing with Father Putt's frightening sermons about Satan's power, fourteen-year-old Joanna was asked to care for a dying man named Follard, whose wife was utterly exhausted by her attempts to care for him during his terminal illness. Throughout the night, young Joanna stayed alone with the dying man, who was convinced that the devil in the form of a great black hound was waiting for him just outside the window of the sickroom. Follard shook so violently and convulsively for over an hour before he died that the bed quaked and vibrated on the floor. As his ravings died away into silence and the vibrations ceased, Joanna realized that he was dead. Follard's traumatic deathbed experience so impressed Joanna that she became convinced of the reality and formidable power of Satan as a paranormal evil entity.

The turbulent historical background to Joanna Southcott's life may have played a significant part in her strange prophecies that began in 1792. The French Revolution and its immediate aftermath worried Britain. Tom Paine (1737–1809) published his famous book *The Rights of Man* in 1791. To add to the general unrest, Richard Brothers, a young naval officer, was uttering wild apocalyptic prophecies about Judgment Day. He believed that the Jews were about to regain the Holy Land in the Middle East, that the British were descended from one of the Lost Tribes of Israel, and that Christ was about to return in power and glory. Brothers was certified insane and restrained in a secure mental hospital for more than ten years.

Southcott's apocalyptic visions and what she thought of as prophetic dreams began about the same time. She reported hearing a voice – as Joan of Arc had done centuries before. It told her that God had woken from sleep and was about to shake the Earth. Joanna went through a time of doubt and mental conflict concerning the *origin* of the voice. At first she thought that Satan was deceiving her and pretending to be God. Then several of her prophecies began to come true, and she thought that the voice might be divine after all and not a satanic delusion. She asked the voice to give her a sign – very much as Gideon had done in Judges 6:36-40. Joanna's sign was duly given in the form of three knocks on her bedstead. She also discovered a talent for producing automatic writing. Her fulfilled prophecies included the death of the apparently fit and healthy Bishop of Exeter, the failure of Lord Malmesbury's peace mission to Paris in 1796, and the French conquest of Italy. These successes convinced Southcott that her voice came from God, not from Satan.

When she was speaking at a religious gathering in Leeds she expressed her view that Satan was responsible for all the evil going on in the world. A member of the audience stood up and heckled her, saying that evil was the result of the disobedience of Adam and Eve. Joanna argued vehemently that God himself had spoken with her and told her that evil came from Satan. Her heckler disagreed, and Joanna told him to leave. She said he was an associate of the devil, and asked her friends in the audience to remove him, which they did. Joanna then declared that he was the enemy of humanity and a friend of the devil.

Another more serious episode concerned the deaths of two men who had set out for Leeds with the intention of confronting Joanna. They died on the way, and she proudly proclaimed that the Angel of Death had intervened on her behalf and punished them for their insolence!

In 1794, Joanna told her followers that the voice had told her that she had been selected to fulfil the prophecy in the book of Revelation 12:1-6. This extract refers to "a woman clothed with the sun, and the moon under her feet, and upon her head a crown of twelve stars." It goes on to say that the woman is due to give birth to a male child who will "rule all nations with a rod of iron." There is also a "great red dragon, having seven heads and ten horns, and seven crowns upon his heads." This satanic beast waits to devour the child as soon as it is born. God intervenes, however, and rescues the child while the woman escapes into the wilderness.

The mysterious voice told her that she had been selected to be the Bride of the Lamb, the woman described in Revelation. A turning point in her career came when the Reverend T.P. Foley, an academic Cambridge clergyman and a former supporter of the mentally ill Richard Brothers, transferred his support to her. Foley and his friend William Sharp, another Brothers supporter, put a number of Joanna's writings into a box, which was then secured with seven seals. It was destined to become a centre of interest for the next two centuries!

Another clergyman who took Joanna's attention was the Reverend Joseph Pomeroy, vicar of the church in the village of St. Kew in Cornwall, England. Her emotions toward him were a strange mix: initially she admired him and felt great affection for him, but after he had burned a number of her letters and papers she turned against him and denounced him as being like King Jehoiakim, who had burned the scroll of prophecies written by Jeremiah (Jeremiah 36:23). She felt that he was then under the same curse as the unfortunate Jehoiakim (635-597 B.C.).

Joanna Southcott's numerous writings include a publication entitled *Dispute Between the Woman and the Powers of Darkness August 3rd 1802*. In this document, she sets out her conversation both with an entity called Satan's Friend and then with Satan himself. A brief extract illustrates the character of this work:

> **Satan's Friend:** But do not charge Satan foolishly, to say, he was the author of all evil.
> **Joanna:** To whom must I ascribe evil, when our Saviour said, Sin was of the Devil, and his works sinners did do? Now if Satan be of my spirit, he will love the Lord with all his heart, and fall down before the Most High God.
> **Satan's Friend:** Is this thy spirit? Then I tell thee thou art lost forever. God has forsaken thee.

Shortly before her death in 1814, at the age of sixty-four, Joanna was convinced that as the Woman from the book of Revelation she was pregnant with a new messiah, to be known as Shiloh. Her thoughts became increasingly crazed and confused, and she regarded herself as a divine or semi-divine being. During some of her rare rational moments she seemed able to accept that she had been hopelessly self-deceived, or deceived by Satan. In some of her worst visions she dreamt of the devil in the form of a pig with its mouth tied; at other times she thought she was battling with him physically, scratching his face and biting off his fingers.

Joanna's many strange experiences illustrate her belief that Satan was very much a paranormal entity and not a personification or a focal point of abstract thoughts. Her ideas run in parallel with what theistic Satanists believe.

Other ideas about the origins of evil, the nature of Satan or Lucifer and the fallen angels, can be traced through the mysterious old *Book of Enoch*. Some scholars regard it as relatively recent, dating back only to the first or second century B.C. Others consider that it is far older, and that Enoch is a genuinely antediluvian hero from some ten or eleven millennia ago.

In the *Book of Enoch*, two hundred Watchers (paranormal flying entities tantamount to angels) rebel and come to Enoch's area of the Middle East. Here, fascinated by the beauty of the local girls, they take them as wives and produce offspring. Whoever the Watchers may really have been, their children are not normal human beings. They are described as "giants," but the term may not refer literally to vast physical size. It may mean that they were gigantic in power or intellect — attributes that the author of Enoch sees as giving them enormous advantages over their human contemporaries. The *Book of Enoch* describes how these rebellious Watchers who mated with terrestrial girls also taught Enoch's people metal-working and the use of herbs. Were these culinary, medicinal, or *magical* herbs?

An extract from Chapter 8 of the *Book of Enoch* describes these things in detail:

> **8:1** Azazel taught men to make swords, daggers, shields and breastplates. He also showed them how to make bracelets and other ornaments, and the art of using

cosmetics for their eyes and decorating their eyelids. He also taught them about jewels and coloured dyes. This changed their world.

8:2 There was much wickedness and fornication: men went astray, and all things were corrupted.

8:3 Amezarak taught them how to cast spells and how to find roots. Armaros showed them how to break spells, and Baraqiel taught them astrology. Kokabiel taught them to read omens, and Asradel taught them the secrets of the movements of the Moon.

For Satanist theory, this raises the important question — assuming there is a factual, historical basis to the *Book of Enoch* — of who the Watchers really were, and where they came from. Could they have been extraterrestrials, technocrats from the lost lands of Atlantis or Lemuria, or travellers from other probability tracks or unknown dimensions?

The very interesting and multi-talented Tony "Doc" Shiels is a professional conjuror, artist, and author with a notorious sense of humour and a profound interest in the paranormal, especially magic and cryptozoology. His investigations have included the strange Owlman seen in Mawnan Woods in Cornwall, England, in 1976. According to Shiels's reports, two young girls saw the Owlman, which they described as "a large winged creature," flying above the tower of Mawnan Church. The frightened girls told their father, and he contacted Shiels, who carried out some investigations in the area.

Other cryptozoologists have compared the Cornish Owlman reports to accounts of a similar phenomenon in the United States known as Mothman. The core of the witnesses' reports describe it as a winged humanoid figure resembling an owl, but having burning red eyes and claws like pincers. Some groups of Satanists and black magicians consider the possibility that the phenomenon is actual a jinn or demonic entity of some type.

How does this contribute to the current analysis of Satanism? Are there groups of Satanists who believe that such demonic manifestations exist? If they do, what is their purpose? Do they mean to instill fear into the witnesses? Do they intend to make contact with humans in order to bring them over into the Satanist camp?

What strange magical secrets did Enoch's people learn from the winged Watchers?

Does this tie in with the very odd reports in the *Book of Enoch*? Were the mysterious winged Watchers that Enoch reported in fact paranormal entities similar to Owlman and Mothman? Shiels himself said when conducting his investigation that the thing seen in the trees and over the church at Mawnan appeared primarily to young girls, just as the Watchers had been attracted to the young girls in Enoch's country.

Satanism, then, can be broadly divided into its theistic and atheistic forms, although there are several other varieties and subdivisions which come to prominence in groups of Satanists who are especially interested in using magic, spells, curses, enchantments, witchcraft, wizardry, and sorcery.

SATAN IN THE ABRAHAMIC RELIGIONS

At their best, in their truest, purest forms, the three great Abrahamic religions — Judaism, Christianity, and Islam — all share benign moral and ethical teachings. In their finest form they teach that a loving, merciful, creating, and sustaining God wills the welfare and happiness of his creation. Reduced to its simplest, essential minimum, the core of all the Abrahamic religions teaches that human beings should love one another and express that love with unselfish kindness, generosity, help, toleration, mercy, and forgiveness. They preach the concepts of caring for others for the sake of a God who loves us all, and then treating them as we, ourselves, would like to be treated. It is diametrically opposed to the satanic principles of ruthless, self-centred, unbounded ambition, relentless greed, desperate hunger for power, and the unlimited search for pleasure.

How do the main Abrahamic religions teach their followers to cope with satanic temptation?

Judaism focuses particularly on the idea that Satan is *not* a rebellious, fallen angel, but an obedient angel with a special mission and purpose under God's direction. In order to understand this Jewish idea, it has to be accepted that God's will for human beings is for them to be free and independent, able to *choose* whether to do good or evil.

Satan then fits into the picture as an angel who is sent to tempt people — to provide opportunities for them to choose good or evil.

In the King James Version of the book of Deuteronomy 30:15, God is recorded as saying: "See, I have set before thee this day life and good, and death and evil." The book of the prophet Isaiah 45:7 contains much the same, where God says: "I form the light, and create darkness; I make peace, and create evil; I the Lord do all these things."

Scholarly Rabbi Tovia Singer is on record as saying that every searching soul in the world is confronted by the choice between good and evil. Singer believes that this is the Almighty's plan for creation: virtue is attained when a person makes a decision to avoid evil and choose good. This Jewish position differs significantly from the traditional Christian reluctance to accept the idea that God could have created Satan as an angel of evil from the beginning. A widely held — though far from universal — Christian view is that Satan was among the highest-ranking angels, but that he was ambitious, rebellious, and disobedient to God. This area of Christian theology contends that a totally benign God did not create Satan to be evil; the evil came from Satan's own mutinous conduct.

This particular Christian slant on the origin of evil is not far away from the dualism of Persian Zoroastrianism, in which the evil and chaotic Ahriman opposes Ahura Mazda, the god of goodness and order. There are some academic religious historians, including Rabbi Singer, who would venture to suggest that the Christian view of Satan as a once-powerful, high-ranking angel who rebelled against Yahweh was actually derived from what Zoroaster taught in the sixth century B.C. The theological problem with the concept of Satan as a rebellious or mutinous angel is that if he was *intended* to be good and obedient, and was *created* to be good and obedient, his fall from grace might suggest that God had created something imperfect or defective.

This can, perhaps, be countered by the recurring idea of the importance of free will in the divine plan. If God wants human beings to be free to choose good independently because they genuinely *want* to be good, why shouldn't angels have an equal freedom of choice? The idea that Satan was an imperfect or defective creation — irreconcilable with the concept of God as Absolute Perfection — is then negated. The angel Satan can still be seen as a perfect creation, but an essential part of his perfection was genuine free will and independence. Satan's wrong decision does not imply any failure on God's part; it simply illustrates God's absolute honesty in creating true freedom of choice.

The Jewish position differs significantly from Christian thinking at this juncture. If Satan is regarded as God's agent in tempting human beings, in giving them a real test, a genuine choice between good and evil, then he is not himself evil, he is merely carrying out God's commands in this particular sphere of moral and ethical activity.

It is interesting to note, as Rabbi Singer does, that the Hebrew word for angel is *malach*, which translates as "messenger." This corresponds to the Greek word *angelos*, which also means "messenger" and is the root of the English word *angel*. These angelic messengers, including Satan, according to Jewish thinking and the Jewish scriptures, always carry out God's will. None of them ever opposes God's will; none of them ever disobeys him.

This explanation of Satan as the angel with the special responsibility of testing people is lucidly expressed in the book of Job. Satan argues that Job's piety and devotion to God is the result of Job's prosperity and large family — of great importance to a Jew of Job's time. He also enjoys excellent health. God gives Satan (at this stage called *the* Satan, meaning the office or role of "accuser" rather than a personal name) permission to take away the things that matter to Job, including his family, who are killed when they are together in the eldest brother's house, which collapses when a great storm blows in from the wilderness.

Later, Job's health is seriously affected as well, but he still battles through all his suffering and loss and refuses to "curse God." In the end all is restored to him and he is wealthier than before.

In the version of the book of Job in the Christian Bible, Job has ten more children to replace the ones who died when the house collapsed on them. According to Rabbi Nahmanides, also known as Ramban (1194-1270), Job's sons and daughters were carried away as captives — not killed by a collapsing house — and were duly restored to him alive and well when they were released.

Although the King James/Authorized Version (KJV/AV) of the Bible, dating from 1611, gives the correct translation for the Hebrew word *rah*, meaning "evil," in Isaiah 45:7, the New International Version of the Bible (NIV) dating from 1978 does not. The word *disaster* was used instead. The NIV verse reads: "I form the light and create darkness, I bring prosperity and create *disaster*; I, the Lord, do all these things."

Was this amendment made, as Rabbi Singer suggests, to distance God from the concept of evil? The AV quite clearly states that God is responsible for evil — the NIV takes a different position.

Early Jewish apocryphal writings provide two accounts of Satan's origin. In the first of these he was created, as Eve was, on the sixth day.

This fits in with the general tradition that Satan was implicated in the Fall of Man. According to the second version, Satan and Sammael are one and the same entity, and Satan is a fallen angel.

According to Talmudic lore, Sammael both appeared as the serpent in Eden and later seduced Eve and impregnated her with Cain, the murderer. He is also said to have taken on Lilith, the screech-owl demoness, as his wife after she had left Adam, and his name is also linked with Na'amah and other angels associated with sacred prostitution.

Sammael is also credited with being the guardian angel that protected Esau, and later became a guardian of the Roman Empire.

There are conflicting and contradictory Hebrew accounts of his personality: some make him good, others evil. In a number of seemingly paradoxical stories he is both! Some versions equate him with the angel of death; others rank him among the most powerful entities in the seventh heaven.

Sammael was supposed to be the angel who wrestled with Jacob, as well as the angel who prevented Abraham from killing his son Isaac. These conflicting examples make it difficult to understand the character and role of Satan in Judaism, if Satan and Sammael are regarded as the same entity.

Other Hebrew scholars and rabbis identify Satan in two distinct ways. In the first, which accords to some extent with the ideas of atheistic Satanism, he is reckoned to be Yetzer ha Rah — the evil impulses *inside* human beings. He is also seen as an independent, objective paranormal entity *outside* human beings. This is in accordance with the ideas of theistic Satanists.

The persistent Hebrew idea of Satan as an opponent or an adversary can be seen several times in the Jewish Torah, where the word *Satan* can refer to a military adversary, as in the first book of Samuel 29:4:

> And the princes of the Philistines were wroth with him; and the princes of the Philistines said unto him, Make this fellow return, that he may go again to his place which thou hast appointed him, and let him not go down with us to battle, lest in the battle he be an **adversary** to us: for wherewith should he reconcile himself unto his master? Should it not be with the heads of these men?

It crops up again in this military sense in the first book of Kings 5:4: "But now the LORD my God hath given me rest on every side, so that there is neither adversary nor evil occurrent."

The same concept of the use of the word *Satan* for an opponent or adversary can be found in the legal sense as well as the military context. There is an example of this usage in Psalm 109, verse 6: "Set thou a wicked man over him: and let Satan (*his opponent, his adversary*) stand at his right hand."

Satan is regarded almost sympathetically in some of the old Jewish religious literature, where there is a parable comparing him to a prostitute hired by a king in order to tempt the king's son. The king orders her to do her best to lead the young man into sin, but although she obeys the king's orders, she secretly hopes that she will fail, and that the prince will pass his father's test. The parable sets out to show Satan as a tempter sent by God, but a tempter who secretly hopes to fail to make his target sin.

In Christianity, there are a number of names that are practically interchangeable with Satan. Referring to him as the devil comes from the Middle English word *devel*, which developed from the Old English term *deofol*. Its origin is the Latin word *diabolus*, which the Romans took from the Greek *diabellein*, meaning to speak ill of someone or to slander them. Lucifer is also used as a synonym for Satan or the devil. The fallen angel is referred to as "the son of the dawn" in Isaiah 14:12, thus identifying Satan as Lucifer: "How art thou fallen from heaven, O Lucifer, son of the morning! How art thou cut down to the ground, which didst weaken the nations!"

Satan is also referred to as Beelzebub on occasion, but Beelzebub was originally an old Philistine god, with *Baal* as one of the name's root words. *Baal-Zebub* simply means "lord of the flies," although the New Testament uses it more or less as a synonym for Satan.

The Divine Comedy, written by Dante Alighieri (1265-1321), renders the name as Belzeboub. He is named as one of the seven princes of hell.

There is an early reference to him in the second book of Kings 1:2:

> And Ahaziah fell down through a lattice in his upper chamber that was in Samaria, and was sick: and he sent messengers, and said unto them, Go, enquire of

> Baalzebub the god of Ekron whether I shall recover of this disease.

The Prophet Elijah says that Ahaziah will die of his injuries for consulting Baalzebub of Ekron instead of consulting Yahweh. Sure enough, Ahaziah dies.

In Mark's Gospel 3:22, the Scribes accuse Jesus of casting out devils by using the power of Beelzebub, the prince of devils: "And the scribes which came down from Jerusalem said, He hath Beelzebub, and by the prince of the devils casteth he out devils."

Christ's superb answer to their accusations is recorded in Matthew's Gospel 12:25-28:

> And Jesus knew their thoughts, and said unto them, Every kingdom divided against itself is brought to desolation; and every city or house divided against itself shall not stand: And if Satan cast out Satan, he is divided against himself; how shall then his kingdom stand? And if I by Beelzebub cast out devils, by whom do your children cast them out? Therefore they shall be your judges. But if I cast out devils by the Spirit of God, then the kingdom of God is come unto you.

Beelzebub was used instead of Beelzeboul in the Syriac translation, as well as in the Latin Vulgate. The Vulgate was the fourth-century version of the bible in Latin and was mainly the work of Jerome (A.D. 347-420) on the instructions of Pope Damasus I (A.D. 305-384). Jerome's work came to be known as *versio vulgata*, meaning the common translation. It later became the official Latin version used by the Roman Catholic Church. More modern translations have reverted to the use of Beelzeboul. Either or both styles – Beelzebub and Beelzeboul – may have been used for an individual person, or persons, or reserved exclusively for deities.

Important archaeological discoveries at Ras Shamra, Syria, known as the ancient seaport city of Ugarit more than three thousand years ago, have shed light on the use of the suffix *zeboul* to indicate a prince or very high-ranking nobleman.

The book entitled the *Testament of Solomon* is classed as pseudepigraphic literature — that is, works attributed to some great and important figure of the past such as Solomon, Elijah, or Nimrod the Mighty Hunter. The *Testament of Solomon* was written at some time during the first and third centuries A.D., and is mainly an index of demons and magical techniques, plus the summoning of appropriate angels who deal with the demons listed. Beelzebul crops up in the *Testament of Solomon* as a demonic prince who had formerly been an important angel. He is associated with Hesperus, at one time the name of the evening star (really the planet Venus as it appears in the evening). Hesperus is brother to Phosphorus (associated with the morning star, the planet Venus as seen in the morning). *Phosphorus* translates from the Greek as "bearer of light" — and "light-bearing," significantly, translates as *lucifer* in Old English! The earliest Greek observers of the heavens thought that the morning and evening stars were two entirely separate celestial bodies, until they picked up the Babylonian observations and accepted that they were one and the same. The planets were duly associated with the gods of classical mythology and what had once been Hesperus/Phosphorus became Aphrodite, Ishtar — or Venus!

The Gospel of Nicodemus, generally included in the New Testament Apocrypha, interchanges the renderings of Beelzebub and Beelzebul more or less at random, but distinguishes between him and Lucifer or Satan as the actual devil.

John Bunyan (1628-88) wrote *Pilgrim's Progress* in 1678 and it includes a reference to Beelzebub: "Beelzebub and them that are with him shoot arrows."

An enlightened occultist, capable of thinking centuries ahead of his time, was the Dutch doctor and demonologist known as Johannes Wier, or Johann Weyer (1515-88). His Latin name was rendered as Ionnes Wierus, and, probably because of his birth sign, Piscinarius. He was opposed to the persecution of witches, and wrote an influential book on the subject called *De Praestigiis Daemonum et Incantationibus ac Venificiis* (The Illusions of the Demons and on Spells and Poisons) which came out in 1563. Two of his later books were also important: both *De Lamiis Liber* (Book on Witches) and *Pseudomonarchia Daemonum* (The False Kingdom of the Demons) appeared in 1577. Johann studied under the great and famous magician and occultist Agrippa (1486-1535), first in Antwerp and later in Bonn, where they were protected by the Prince-Bishop Hermann von Wied (1477-1552). Agrippa died at the age of forty-eight while on a trip to France: the real cause of his death is unknown, but various theories attribute it to dark magic of some sort launched at him by his enemies. He had completed a work on demonology only two years before his death.

Wier practised medicine in Grave and Arnhem, where he gave advice on witchcraft. So enlightened, and so far ahead of his time was he that he is credited with being one of the first to diagnose people who thought that they were practising witchcraft as suffering from a form of mental illness. Wier moved from Arnhem (when they were no longer able to pay his salary as town physician) to Cleves, where he served as court physician to William of Cleves (1516-92), known as William the Rich, brother to Anne of Cleves, who was briefly married to King Henry VIII.

Strangely, in view of his otherwise advanced rational ideas, Wier felt that the devil and his cohorts of demons did have *some* limited power, but that it was not as dangerous as it was thought to be in the traditional Christian views of his time. In Wier's opinion, demons were able to create illusions, and when magicians did so, Wier thought that they were using satanic power to do it. Wier's books contained many detailed instructions about controlling demons by invoking the Name of God and the Holy Trinity. His general hypothesis was that demons could be controlled, and he was also one of the first writers on the topic to use the term *exorcist*.

Weir found himself confronted by Jean Bodin (1530-96) and Thomas Erastus (1524-83) — after whom the heresy of Erastianism is named. Bodin's book, *De la démonomanie des sorciers* (The Demon Mania of Witches), was published in 1580. He saw witchcraft and demonology as a very real threat to society, and his book contained detailed instructions to judges on how to deal effectively with cases of witchcraft.

The Dominican inquisitor Sebastien Michaelis (*circa* 1570-1630), who was responsible for the torture and execution of numerous witchcraft suspects, regarded Beelzebub as one of the top three in the hierarchy of hell. The other two top posts were filled by Lucifer and Leviathan. According to Michaelis, Beelzebub was the demon responsible for tempting mortals into the sin of pride. Other demonologists of the period gave the top three places to Beelzebub, Ashtoreth, and Lucifer. John Milton (1608-74), the author of *Paradise Lost*, put Beelzebub second in the hierarchy of hell. Referring to Beelzebub, Milton wrote: "than whom, Satan except, non higher sat ..."

Peter Binsfeld (or Binsfield), best known by his Latin name of Petrus Binsfeldius (1545-98), was a German bishop and theologian who associated Beelzebub with the sin of gluttony rather than pride. Francis Barrett (*circa* 1770-1830) was an expert occultist and author of an interesting book called *The Magus*. This covered what Barrett thought of as the natural magic in herbs and stones. He was also impressed by alchemy and the power of magnetism. In Barrett's opinion, Beelzebub was a demon of deception and illusion, who tempted people to worship false gods.

In the tragic case of Sister Madeleine de Demandolx de la Palud, a teenaged nun whose wild accusations led to the death at the stake of Father Jean-Baptiste Gaufridi in 1611, it was Beelzebub who had allegedly possessed Madeleine and several other nuns at Aix-en-Provence.

Even worse atrocities occurred at Loudun, and when the unfortunate Urbain Grandier was burned at the stake in 1634, witnesses reported seeing a very large fly buzzing around his head. This was taken as a sure sign that his soul had been taken to hell on the orders of Beelzebub, Lord of the Flies.

Another tragic case concerned two elderly widows from Lowestoft in Suffolk, England, who were tried for witchcraft at Bury St. Edmunds assizes in 1664. Thirteen indictments were brought against them, including the bewitching of children — Anne Durent, Susan Chandler, and Elizabeth Pacy — causing fainting fits, causing victims to vomit up pins, and laming John Sheringham and killing his animals by magic. The two women were Amy Duny and Rose Cullender. Their principal accuser was a merchant and "eminent dissenter" named Samuel Pacy. Samuel believed that his daughters were bewitched and his suspicions fell on Amy Duny. At his request she was placed in the stocks, but his daughters did not improve. He then had both Amy and Rose brought before the courts on the witchcraft charge.

Having been arrested, the women were searched for so-called "witch marks." It was generally believed during the seventeenth century witch mania that witches had a mark where they had been touched or kissed by

Satan when their contracts with him were signed. Any mole or birthmark was enough to get a conviction. It was also believed that those witches who worked with imps or familiars had extra teats from which the imps could draw blood. Any large mole or wart would be enough evidence for the accusers. Rose Cullender had enough marks to be convicted and was sent, with Amy, for trial before Sir Matthew Hale, a circuit judge. It must be remembered that the legal system of seventeenth-century England had few, if any, laws of evidence. The wildest hearsay testimony could be offered and accepted.

The three children were brought in, saw the unfortunate old women and promptly threw screaming fits. They were then removed from the court. Anne Durent's mother gave evidence of her quarrel with Amy Duny as a result of which Amy had warned Mrs. Durent not to anger her. Following this, Mrs Durent said that her son had developed fainting fits and she had called in Dr. Jacob of Yarmouth, who had the reputation of being an expert in curing illnesses brought on by witchcraft. Under his direction, the boy's blanket was hung up near the fire, and a toad was seen near it. Dr. Jacob flung the unfortunate toad into the fire where it exploded loudly. The explosion would not have surprised a biologist, but it surprised the witnesses! The exploding toad was more than enough to convince everyone present that the boy had really been bewitched.

The next evidence came from Jane Bocking and Deborah Pacy, who testified that as a result of being bewitched they were vomiting up pins. It was reported that Amy Duny had tried to buy herrings from the Pacy family, but had been refused. It was after that refusal, according to the family's evidence, that their troubles began. The children were sent to stay with their aunt in Yarmouth, but she was a very sensible and practical woman who suspected childish practical jokes. Accordingly she searched them thoroughly for concealed pins and removed any that she found. Despite all her efforts, they managed to cough up another thirty odd pins! This is particularly interesting in view of the price of pins in the seventeenth century. The phrase "pin money" comes from this time simply because pins were relatively expensive then.

Rose and Amy were *almost* acquitted. Part of the evidence offered against Rose and Amy was that the girls who claimed to be bewitched screamed if Amy or Rose touched them. One very fair-minded and sensible legal officer, Sergeant Keeling, suggested blindfolding the girls and asking innocent bystanders and legal officers to touch them. They screamed every time, regardless of who touched them! Unfortunately, the court called in Dr. Brown from Norwich. Like Dr. Jacob of Yarmouth, Dr. Brown was regarded as an expert on illnesses caused by witchcraft. He quoted similar cases that he had studied in Denmark and assured the court that the children really were bewitched. John Soam, another witness, then turned up and claimed that after his cart had accidentally collided with Amy Duny's house, she had become very angry and bewitched it. It had then overturned on three occasions.

Anne Sandeswell, another prosecution witness, testified that Amy had prophesied that unless a certain chimney in the town was repaired it would collapse. It wasn't — and it did! This accurate prophecy was regarded as evidence of Amy's magical ability. Despite the best efforts of the honest and sensible Sergeant Keeling, the two poor old widows were found guilty, sentenced to death, and hanged.

This kind of tragedy was by no means restricted to England. During the notorious Salem Witch Trials of 1692, when the witchcraft hysteria hit Salem and other towns in Massachusetts, leading to the deaths of many innocent people, the name of Beelzebub again featured prominently in the proceedings. The Reverend Cotton Mather (1663-1728), an influential Puritan minister in New England at the time, wrote a pamphlet entitled *Of Beelzebub and His Plot*.

Canonical Christian writers, such as those responsible for the book of Revelation at the end of the New Testament in the Christian Bible, for the Gospel of John, and for the Epistles to the Ephesians and Corinthians, identify Satan with "the dragon" and "the old serpent." Revelation also calls him "the deceiver." John's Gospel 12:31, refers to him as "the prince of this world" — "Now is the judgment of this world: now shall the prince of this world be cast out."

In Ephesians 2:2, Paul calls him "the prince of the power of the air" — "Wherein in time past ye walked according to the course of this world, according to the prince of the power of the air, the spirit that now worketh in the children of disobedience."

In the second Epistle to the Corinthians 4:4, Paul refers to the devil as "the god of this world" — "In whom the god of this world hath blinded the minds of them which believe not, lest the light of the glorious gospel of Christ, who is the image of God, should shine unto them."

The Christadelphians, who trace their origins to Dr. John Thomas (1805-71), have a view of Satan that is very similar to the old Hebrew idea of him as an adversary. They see him not as a person but as more or less any type of sin and temptation which hinders their spiritual development.

The traditional Christian position regarding Satan or the devil can be summed up under four major headings: his existence, his nature, his powers, and his activities.

From a basic, simplistic, scriptural perspective, something that might be termed a spirit of evil is referred to repeatedly, although by a wide variety of names. Every quality and every action that can be seen as an element of personality is attributed to him repeatedly. Theologically, it is essential for some hypotheses — especially those dealing with the problems of theodicy — that he exists. The great central problem of arguing rationally for or against the devil's existence is that while the *effects* of evil are all too visible in every sphere of life, its *causes* are not. What might be termed by some fundamentalist Christians "the revelation of scripture" points to the absolute supremacy of God, and the *existence* of evil as a mere *subsistence* under God's power and control. The *reason* for its existence, however, remains a matter of conjecture within Christian thinking, especially for academic, liberal modernists.

As great a problem as the existence — or otherwise — of Satan in any personal sense, is the problem of his *nature*. Assuming that he exists, what's he like? There is not too much about his nature and character to be found in Christian scripture. It is possible to conclude in traditional Christian thought that he was originally a very powerful, high-ranking angelic being, a rational being possessing power, intelligence, and energy far above the human level. It then becomes pertinent to ask why, with all that intelligence, he foolishly rebelled against God.

George MacDonald (1824-1905) was a truly great Christian thinker and writer who believed in universal redemption and felt that even Satan would one day return to God. MacDonald's universalism differs significantly from traditional Christian teachings about hell and damnation and the ultimate destruction of Satan.

The character of Satan as described in scripture is that of a murderer, a liar, and a deceitful tempter. There is also reference to him as being immensely proud – the inference being that it was pride that led to his fall.

It may be possible to ascertain a clearer picture of the scriptural attributes of Satan, from a Christian standpoint, by seeing his nature as the opposite of God's. If God's nature can be summarized as love, truth, and holiness (or purity), then Satan's nature can be summarized as hatred, falsehood, and corruption. If restless energy, guile, and craftiness, and an intense desire to spread corruption are added to his nature, the scriptural appraisal of his character is complete.

By what *actions* then does Satan make his presence felt according to Christian scripture? There are some scriptural passages that reveal Satan's *direct* activity in tempting people away from God and goodness; other references suggest that he works by using *instruments* of temptation. Their own inner desire for power, for example, tempts people to behave in evil ways in order to obtain and then retain ever-increasing power. The desire for wealth – often as a route to power – tempts people to cheat and steal.

Master criminals and gang leaders can then be seen to be acting as instruments of Satan in leading others astray.

The *direct* action of Satan himself, his *direct* influence over a human mind and spirit, is sometimes described by traditional Christian thinkers as the influence of his powerful, dynamic evil nature on those who harbour the germ of that same evil. Does it differ from the influence of human "bad company" only in degree, rather than in kind? Is it quantitative rather than qualitative? Does *direct* satanic influence work without having to be expressed in words or in actions? Christian scripture seems to suggest this in the parable of the sower in Matthew 13:19:

> When any one heareth the word of the kingdom, and understandeth it not, then cometh the wicked one, and catcheth away that which was sown in his heart. This is he which received seed by the way side.

The direct satanic influence here is seen as a negative one; it is a removal of the good, rather than an insertion of evil. Another aspect of direct satanic evil is expressed in the parable of the wheat and the tares, in which tares, or weeds, are deliberately sown in a wheat field by an enemy.

The owner of the field tells his workers to allow both to grow together until harvest time.

Matthew 13:39 explains the parable: "The enemy that sowed them is the devil; the harvest is the end of the world; and the reapers are the angels."

The evil influence here is seen as a positive and direct one: evil is described as being deliberately introduced into the world by Satan.

Paul's attitude to evil and Satan's role is made clear when he is explaining Christianity to King Herod Agrippa (10 B.C.-A.D. 44). Paul describes his purpose as a Christian missionary in Acts 26:18: "To open their eyes, and to turn them from darkness to light, and from the power of Satan unto God, that they may receive forgiveness of sins, and inheritance among them which are sanctified by faith that is in me."

Islamic teaching about Satan in the Holy Qur'an differs significantly from Jewish and Christian concepts. The Arabic term *Shaitan*, which is the equivalent of Satan, comes from an adjectival root-word meaning "distant, far away, astray." *Shaitan* is sometimes translated as "devil." In its adjectival form, *Shaitan* can be applied either to a human being or one of the jinn. The actual personal name of the devil in the Genesis equivalent in the Holy Qur'an is Iblis. He was given an order from Allah to bow down to Adam, but refused on the grounds that he was a superior being: Adam having been made from clay, while he, Iblis, a powerful jinn rather than an angelic being, had been made from fire. Unlike the angels, in Islamic tradition, the jinn can exercise free will just as human beings can. The point is clearly expressed in the Holy Qur'an 2:34: "And when we said to the angels: Make obeisance to Adam; they made obeisance but Iblis (did it not). He was of the jinn, so he transgressed the commandment of his Lord."

Iblis was punished by being forced out of heaven to await further retribution on Judgment Day. Iblis then became more widely known as *Shaitan*, a name that was given the modified meaning of "enemy," "rebel," or "devil." He is referred to as Iblis some eleven times in the Holy Qur'an and as Shaitan close to ninety times. He declared that if his punishment was to be deferred until Judgment Day, he would spend the intervening time corrupting as many of Adam's descendants as he could.

After tempting Adam and Eve to eat the forbidden fruit, Iblis, alias Shaitan (Satan), was sent to Earth with them.

Adam and Eve and the serpent.

In Islamic theology, Shaitan and his followers are sometimes known as *whisperers*. They are said to speak very quietly put persistently into people's minds and hearts, urging them to think evil thoughts, to say evil words, and to perform evil deeds. According to Islamic teaching this constant whispering by the devil and his followers is the source of the human desire to commit sin. To counteract this, and to protect God's people from evil and its consequences, the Holy Qur'an provides special prayers to help the faithful to overcome what Shaitan and his minions continuously whisper. This passage is found in the Holy Qur'an 114:1-6:

> In the name of Allah, the Compassionate, the Merciful.
> Say: I seek refuge in the Lord of mankind,
> The King of mankind,
> The God of mankind,
> From the evil of the sneaking whisperer Shaitan,
> Who whispers in the hearts of mankind,
> Of the jinn and of mankind.

Jahannam is hell in Islam, and the Islamic belief is that Shaitan will be cast into it at the end of time along with all who have followed his sinful teachings. Those who have been successful in their resistance to him with the help of Allah will enjoy the endless delights of *Jannah*, the Islamic paradise. The view of Shaitan is that he does not, however, function outside the control of Allah, who is absolutely supreme and sovereign over the whole universe. Shaitan hates humanity and launches all his attacks against it. Islam, therefore, warns people to do all in their power, with Allah's help, to fight against the temptations that Shaitan whispers inside their minds.

Another difference between jinn and angels in Islamic thought is that the jinn experience physical needs and wants, and can, in exceptional circumstances, be killed. They are not, however, limited by many of the constraints that limit human activities. They are largely malevolent and mischievous, and frequently cause accidents and disease for humans. These accidents and diseases are preventable when appropriate prayers for protection are made to Allah. Certain magical rites are also felt to guard the user against the evils threatened by the jinn.

The concept of the jinn is an important one, and formed an essential part of the cultural background in the Middle East for many pre-Islamic centuries. The famous *Thousand and One Arabian Nights* can be traced back at least to the eighth century A.D. King Shahryar had been deceived by his new queen, who was executed for her infidelity. The embittered monarch then married a long series of beautiful virgin wives, each of whom was executed on the day after her bridal night with Shahryar. At last, he married Scheherazade, daughter of his vizier, who protected her life by telling the king stories that always broke off at an exciting point in the narrative, and so he let her live one more day in order to finish the tale that had intrigued him. After 1,001 such stories, Shahryar realized that he loved her, and all ideas of execution were dropped. The stories told during the 1,001 nights frequently included jinn among their intriguing characters. The origins of these stories could be traced from Arabia, Persia, India, Mesopotamia, and Egypt. Many of them were popular folktales from the era of the Caliphate.

Although Shaitan and the lesser shaitans are evil spirits in modern Islam, in pre-Islamic culture they were thought of as being rather like the

Greek idea of daemons. They were believed to provide insight and ideas for seers, prophets, mediums, and fortune tellers. In this capacity, jinn were capable of doing good as well as evil.

The three great Abrahamic religions share certain ideas about good and evil, and about Satan and his minions. In all three faiths, the absolute goodness and power of God is central. The reasons for Satan's rebellion differ slightly, as does the degree of power and influence he is able to exert against human beings. The true believer's defence against Satan – and his minions – under God's protection is complete.

There are some variations of thought as to what will become of Satan and the fallen angels, or disobedient jinn, on Judgment Day. On the whole, however, there is a worthwhile consensus among the three faiths: the power and goodness of God; the role of Satan as the source of evil and the source of temptation to do evil; and, finally, the ultimate triumph of good and the complete overthrow of evil at the end of all things.

The Identity, Character and Nature of Satan

The range of ideas about Satan is great. Religious fundamentalists and traditionalists would probably see him as a personalized entity, self-aware and self-motivated, or as a corrupted member of the jinn or a rebellious angel. Perhaps they even see him as an obedient but adversarial angel such as he is portrayed in the book of Job.

A secular psychologist or psychiatrist might look for explanations involving a guilt complex and the subject's attempt to shift the blame for any unacceptable behaviour by saying that Satan tempted him to do it. There is a well-known statuary group portraying the aftermath of eating the forbidden fruit in Eden in which the hand of God is pointing at Adam, Adam is pointing at Eve, and she is pointing at the serpent. When war criminals are being tried, they all attempt to blame one another, and the pathetic cry goes up: "I was only obeying orders." Having someone else to blame — especially a powerful, paranormal entity like Satan — does provide a certain element of relief from guilt.

Medical science might regard visions of Satan and his attendant demons as hallucinations caused by brain infection, tumours, cerebral blood clots, or other trauma.

Speculative explanations could include categorizing Satan and the demons as extraterrestrial visitors with powers greatly in excess of those of normal, earthly humanity. Such extraterrestrials with plans of world domination would happily encourage simplistic religious beliefs to camouflage their real identity. What if two rival groups of extraterrestrials arrived more or less simultaneously in the remote past? Suppose that genetic engineering went on in Eden. The cloning of Eve from one of Adam's ribs harmonizes with such a theory. One group would probably describe the other as "evil." The expulsion from Eden could be interpreted as removing contaminated specimens from a protected environment to prevent further contamination.

The Identity, Character, and Nature of Satan

Satan as a rebellious jinn or fallen angel.

Other hypotheses would see these "visitors" not as extraterrestrials from some distant planet but as highly advanced technologists, survivors from Atlantis or Lemuria, still intent on dominating the rest of us. Yet other theories consider the possibility of time-travellers, or interdimensional travellers — strange beings from the "Worlds of If."

After the strange *tulpa* experiences of Alexandra David-Néel in Tibet, the possibility of Satan and the demons as thought-forms created by the dark ideas in the depths of the human mind is also worth considering. Can thinking of evil — at a conscious level, like a magician casting dark spells, or at a subconscious level, like the malevolent thoughts that even the saintliest people suppress and deny — actually *create* evil entities like Satan and the demons?

The 1956 sci-fi film *Forbidden Planet* incorporated the idea of *tulpa*-type monsters emerging from the subconscious mind.

In his Letter to the Philippians 4:8, Paul very wisely advocated positive, wholesome thinking:

> Finally, brethren, whatsoever things are true, whatsoever things are honest, whatsoever things are just, whatsoever things are pure, whatsoever things are lovely, whatsoever things are of good report; if there be any virtue, and if there be any praise, think on these things.

With this vast range of widely divergent possibilities to consider, if Satan exists, what is his true identity? What sort of character is he? What is his real nature? The possibilities need to be explored separately, in depth and in detail.

Suppose first that he is a real, independent, self-aware, superhuman entity endowed with free will and genuine *choice*. Suppose, too, that he once exercised that freedom of choice to defy and disobey God. This satanic entity then seems to have emotive thought as well as cognitive thought. His actions suggest that he is proud and ambitious. He wants to be independent. He wants to express himself. Pride, ambition, and the desire for unencumbered self-expression are then part of his nature. But what was the *reason* for his initial disobedience and rebellion? Was it something to do with jealousy over the creation of human beings? Is that why the common factor in all evil is to cause pain and suffering for human beings? Just as love can be analyzed as the unfailing desire to bring happiness to those who are loved, can evil be analyzed as the persistent desire to harm those who are hated?

It is difficult enough to get inside the minds and to unravel the motivations of other human beings like ourselves. It is infinitely more difficult — if not totally impossible — to get inside the mind of a being such as Satan. If he exists, and if he is some sort of fallen angel or corrupt jinn, he is almost certainly vastly more intelligent than the most brilliant human. How can a well-meaning chimpanzee get inside the thoughts of Albert Einstein or Nicola Tesla? How can the best psychologist, philosopher, or theologian get inside the mind of Satan? How can we guess at his motivations, at what he really thinks, at what he really wants?

What does Satan really *want?*

Would the kind of enmity that the traditional religious Satan allegedly feels toward humanity make him want to maximize human suffering, or simply to destroy us? In his brilliant book *The Screwtape Letters* C.S. Lewis suggests that Screwtape and the other demons actually feed on human misery and suffering.

But is there *more* to Satan's complex nature than the desire to inflict suffering and death on human beings? Does he want things for himself? And if he does, what *are* those things? Perhaps he hopes for reinstatement as a jinn or an angel, or reconciliation with God and resumption of his original role in the angelic hierarchy.

Examining human ambition as a motivating force within certain people might provide a clue, however inadequate. The person who desires money attains a few hundred thousand, and then wants millions. Having obtained ten million, he wants a hundred million, then a billion, and so on. Does ambition work like that on the grand scale, as well? If Satan seeks power, how much power does he seek? Does he wish to replace God as Lord of the Universe? If that is his ultimate objective, what are his intermediate strategies?

What if he is not a rebellious or disobedient super-human entity, but a totally obedient one, carrying out God's wishes by testing people as Job was tested? What if Satan is merely adversarial in the sense that the counsel for the prosecution is merely fulfilling a role in court as part of the judicial process? Then his motivation is entirely different, and like a good legal officer he obeys the judge and follows the legal procedures pertinent to his role in the court.

The girl in the parable of the prostitute sent by the king to tempt the prince secretly hopes that he will withstand her temptations. In much the same way, the Satan as the God-appointed adversary secretly hopes that the person being tempted will resist all his temptations and so meet God's moral and ethical standards. If this is the correct interpretation of the nature of the Satan, then he is just as much an angel of God, doing God's will, as an angel whose task it is to bring healing, health, comfort after sadness, or fresh inspiration to do some great good work for the benefit of others. If the Satan is a loyal and obedient angel, his only motivation will be to carry out God's will to the very best of his ability and at all times.

What if Satan is not an angel, loyal or rebellious? What else might he be if he exists? Is it possible that he could be an extraterrestrial visitor of some kind?

The universe is vast. Modern cosmology reveals ever greater dimensions and ever greater mysteries beyond them. If only one star in a hundred had a planetary system ... and if only one planet in a hundred had the conditions to support life as we know it ... and if only one in a hundred of those potentially life-supporting planets had intelligent life on it ... and if only one in a hundred of those had intelligent life *with space travel technology* ... there would still be many thousands of potential extraterrestrial visitors out there!

Suppose that some of these visitors wanted to take over our Earth, to control and develop us so that we would be of use to them. Imagine that there are two or three different rival groups, all with similar ambitions. Was the Garden of Eden a genetic engineering centre? Were Adam and Eve created by beings from another planet, or drastically modified by them from simpler life forms already extant here? Was Eve cloned from Adam's rib? Could fear of contamination from a rival group of technologically

Was Satan a genetic engineer? If so, what was he trying to make?

advanced beings have led to the expulsion from Eden? Who or what was the serpent? Was he a member of one of the rival groups?

If Satan was just the name given by extraterrestrial group A to a member, or members, of extraterrestrial group B, it would signify nothing more than that he was a rival, and that "good" human beings should avoid him and ignore whatever he said to them.

If we assume that neither of the rival groups was more or less moral than the other, and that both wanted to exploit whatever resources Earth and its inhabitants had to offer, then the motivations of both parties were more or less similar, and their ethics and morality were similar, as well. There is not then a contest or conflict between "good" and "evil" but rather a contest between colonizers from different planets. The motivations of both would be much the same: defeat the opposition and make the most of what Earth has to offer. It is, of course, equally possible that one group *might* have had high moral principles and have been concerned about protecting our ancestors from exploitation — or worse — thus allowing them to develop independently.

If the speculation is extended to rival groups of highly advanced humanoids who have survived since the legendary days of Atlantis and Lemuria, then perhaps we have a very ancient situation in which Lemurians and Atlanteans are struggling against each other — or struggling against extraterrestrials. Perhaps the situation is one in which humans (including Lemurians and Atlanteans) are matched against extraterrestrials. There are several possible scenarios involving various permutations of allies and enemies.

Reverting to the hypothesis of cloning and genetic engineering, which began with the creation of Eve from Adam's rib, is it remotely possible that the Pan figure of ancient mythology — part man, part goat, like the traditional Satan image — was the product of genetic engineering?

If that possibility can be considered, does the centaur of mythology — part man, part horse — come into the same genetically engineered category? The appearance of many jinn and demons in half-human form can then, perhaps, also be "explained" in terms of genetic engineering. As an explanation for the appearance of Satan and his minions — and the ways in which they are described in religious texts, myths, and legends — it is way out on the periphery. Yet the immortal advice of Charles

Were Pan and the Centaur products of genetic engineering?

Hoy Fort (1874–1932) still stands: "Nothing is so ridiculous that it need not be investigated and nothing is so firmly proven that it need not be investigated again."

If Satan was *not* a fallen angel, *not* a corrupt member of the jinn, *not* a tulpa, *not* an extraterrestrial, *not* an Atlantean or Lemurian, and *not* a product of genetic engineering, *what might he have been?* It is the most avant-garde of our twenty-first-century physicists who dare to speculate about the probable existence of other dimensions over and above the three dimensions of space and time with which we are familiar. If other dimensions *do* exist, was Satan from one of them, rather than from another planet? There is also the possibility of time travel. Did he come *somehow* from an indeterminate future, or from some remote eon of the distant past when beings of his ilk existed?

There are also the so-called "Worlds of If" — the probability tracks that appeal to innovative physicists in the same way that additional dimensions do. Suppose, for argument's sake, that you *missed* a particular train or bus which then crashed. In our track of "real" existence, you are still here: very much alive and well. On the probability track where you *caught* the train or bus that was involved in a horrendous accident, you might be dead, or very badly injured. Think of another probability track where you won a million on the lottery, and our real-life track where you are still working hard for a living. What if — as some physicists dare to theorize — it might be possible to move *between* probability tracks and go to live on a different World of If?

It has been theorized that the entities described as Lucifer, Satan, Beelzebub, and their accompanying demons are actually beings from a very strange, parallel world, a probability track where things worked out very differently from the way they did in what we like to think of as our normal, everyday "reality." What witches, wizards, enchanters, and sorcerers think of as "magic" may simply be ways of opening a portal between the probability tracks so that demons from a bizarre alternative reality are able to get through into what we think of as our "normal" or "real" world.

What might be the *motivations* of such beings once they enter our "reality"? Would they endeavour to modify our reality so that it bore a closer resemblance to their probability track — the *alternative* reality — from which they had come? From the point of view of human beings like us who were acclimatized to our reality, would it seem that what the visitors were trying to do was wrong or "evil"? Would they endeavour to create additional portals so that movement between the parallel universes became easier? Would they seek somehow to *blend* the two tracks into one single reality within which entities from our world and theirs are able to intermingle freely and easily?

One hypothesis does not necessarily *exclude* another. For the theist, the Supreme God of goodness, the creating and sustaining God of *every* universe, is inescapably also the God of every probability track. The demonic refugees from an alternative reality — another World of If — into our world, may equally well have been rebellious, disobedient jinn or fallen angels on the parallel world from which they came. Does their motivation then remain constant? If they disobeyed God on their original world, would they simply go on attempting to disobey him on our world, and to cause trouble here by tempting human beings to perform evil?

If Satan and the demons are nonexistent in any real objective sense, then any analysis of their nature and their motivations transfers to the human minds from which they sprang and in which they "live." They are nothing more than the repressed thoughts and feelings that "normal" people find it too difficult to face up to. Just as the patient with an enormous inferiority complex tries to compensate for it by behaving in a dominant, boastful, and aggressive way to demonstrate superiority, so the person with a subconscious mind filled with deep, dark, evil urges seeks to demonstrate altruism, goodness, integrity, kindness, and unselfishness. A subconscious mind filled with repressed desires to rape, murder, dominate, and terrify others in what might be styled a demonic fashion, may camouflage those repressed desires by trying to appear unusually kind, generous, and helpful to others. It might then be possible to argue that purely mental demons which do not exist in any real or objective sense are nevertheless capable of motivation. Their twin motivations are to disguise themselves by appearing "good" at a superficial, observable level while subconsciously desiring to commit selfish and brutal acts.

In attempting to assess the possible origin, identity, character, and nature of Satan or Lucifer, we have looked at the possibility that he is an obedient and loyal angel, carrying out God's work of testing people. It is also possible that he is a fallen, or rebellious angel, or perhaps even a jinn. We have examined the possibility that he is an entity from one of the legendary lost lands of Atlantis or Lemuria, who somehow survived their submergence. The possibility that he is an extraterrestrial has also been examined, along with the possibility that, if he *is* of another world, he may have been involved in a genetic engineering project centred on Adam and Eve.

The hypothesis that he came from another time has been looked at, as well. The great difficulty with all time-travel theories, of course, is that the future is not fixed. Tomorrow is produced by the things that are done today. Today is the mould in which the molten possibilities of tomorrow are cast. If Satan is a time-traveller, he can hardly have come from the future — because the future is indeterminate. What if at some remote time in the past there were civilizations of great sophistication and complexity, with technology way ahead of ours but now totally lost to us? Did any of them have time travel? Did the entity we call Satan escape using a time machine from an ancient disaster that overwhelmed one of those ancient civilizations? Yet, if he did, how could he escape into an *indeterminate* future? When all the mere *probabilities* that existed in his ancient time eventually condensed, crystallized, solidified, and settled down to create what we think of as our *reality*, how did he get here? The problem that bedevils all time-travel theory is how a time-traveller can leap forward into a future *that doesn't yet exist* as far as he is concerned.

The parallel universe hypothesis, the probability track theory, has also been examined. If, as some advanced physicists imagine, there are alternative realities — the intriguing Worlds of If — is it possible that Satan came from one of those?

His existence as a *tulpa*, or thought form, has also been considered, along with his nonexistence in any objective state. If he is only a repressed image in the human subconscious, how can he be detected there, and what are the secret motives of the people in whose subconscious minds he dwells?

II

Satanic Worship and Ritual

Satanic worship and ritual varies widely both in its form and in the number of Satanists taking part at any one time. A devil-worshipper can perform his satanic service entirely alone, solely for his own purposes. There is no need for a satanic priest or guru to be present in order for the service to take place. When a solo service or ritual of this type is being conducted, the individual Satanist becomes his own priest, or officiant. In the strictest sense, the only essential ingredient of a satanic service is the individual Satanist who is conducting it. Theoretically, it can take place *anywhere* — including the inside of the Satanist's mind, as he is serving behind the counter, sitting at the computer keyboard, relaxing at home, or driving to work through rush-hour traffic.

On most occasions, candles and an altar are helpful accessories, but they are not essential. There are no rules or regulations, as such, about the precise ways that every satanic service has to be conducted. Freedom and independence are of the essence. Some Satanists perform very basic rituals on most occasions — especially when they are alone — but can also perform highly complex rituals in company and for special occasions in the satanic calendar.

In its simplest, non-specific, non-religious sense, the idea of a ritual can imply nothing more than some regular function. If a person always drinks cocoa before going to bed, it can be referred to as the ritual mug of cocoa. Waiting at a particular bus stop for a particular bus at a particular time can also be thought of as a ritual on the part of the person who travels in that way. In its more specialized sense, the term *ritual* relates to the particular, prescribed order of a religious ceremony — regardless of faith or denomination. There can, therefore, be such a thing as a prescribed satanic ritual.

Religious rituals relate to habitual routines and customary practices within a religious context. They are performed with the intention of helping the participants to make contact with the spiritual being or spiritual forces with which they hope to commune. In this most basic and fundamental sense of practising a religious ritual, simply attending church regularly on a Sunday morning is a Christian ritual.

To understand the nature of religious ritual, it is helpful to analyze the *purpose* of it. *Why* am I going to this place at this time? Some people might decide to perform a particular ritual — especially a magical ritual — in order to make certain things happen in a certain way; that is, to make things happen in a way that they *will* those things to happen.

A useful example to illustrate this point is the following spell that is used by a believer in magic who wishes to sell a property:

> **Apparatus and ingredients:** one gold candle; one red candle; lavender oil.
> **Time:** during the waning of the moon on a night when the moon is clearly visible.
> **Method:** Add seven drops of lavender oil to the fuel in your oil-burning lamp. Place the gold candle to the right of the burner and the red candle on the left. Light the gold one first, then the red. Say the following words: "This house sells quickly for [insert the price you want for the house in the incantation at this point]. May it be so." Repeat the spell on the nights during which the moon is waning, and make sure that both candles have burned down completely.

Performing magic in this way to accomplish a set purpose has been likened by Satanists and magicians to becoming, in a sense, your own genie and granting your own wishes. Some dedicated Satanists may add to the spell by calling specifically on Satan's help to ensure that the property is sold quickly and for the price they want.

For some committed Satanists and devil-worshippers, however, religious rituals are focused on what they would describe as spending time communing with Satan, whom they tend to refer to respectfully as the Prince of Darkness, rather than using Satanism merely as a means to enhance their magical rituals. They do not seem to want to achieve simple physical advantages such as selling a house at a good price: they express a wish to get closer to Satan himself. They regard this as a way of committing themselves ever more deeply to the satanic path they have chosen. There is a strange parallel here with the behaviour of deeply religious monks and nuns who withdraw from the world and all worldly desire in order to commune more deeply with God. An extreme example is the ascetic Saint Simeon Stylites (A.D. 390-459) who spent thirty-seven years in deep religious contemplation on top of a pillar near Aleppo in Syria.

So it may be suggested that there are two purposes behind these satanic rituals. The first is simpler, more direct, and more understandable. The satanic ritualist wants something – like a quick sale of his house – and performs a magical spell that invokes Satan's intervention on his behalf. The second, the deeper and more disturbing, is the ritual that draws the devil-worshipper into closer communion with the devil, but has no other purpose than that.

Having analyzed the purpose behind the ritual, the next stage of the analysis is to examine what is actually done during the ritual. The ritualists have to decide what will actually take place in the course of performing their ritual. There are a number of traditional forms that such worship can take. For example, a decision must be made over whether an altar is needed, what form it will take, and where it will be placed. There is also the question of who – or *what* – will be placed on it. Will prayers be said? Will incantations be chanted or sung? Will special notice be taken of the four cardinal points of the compass? How much symbolic imagery will be involved? Might a magical "doll" be used to bring disaster or destruction on an enemy of the Satanists?

Will candles be lit? Will copulation take place if sexual magic is part of the ritual? Will any special robes or headgear be worn? Will any musical effects be used, such as the blowing of horns or the beating of drums? Will charms, talismans, or amulets form part of the ritual?

Some Satanists will play music that they regard as appropriate as a background to their ritual. Others may run what they think of as an extract from an appropriate film, video, or DVD, with the sound muted, as the ritual proceeds. When the film and background music come to an end, the ceremony is concluded.

Satanism and Demonology

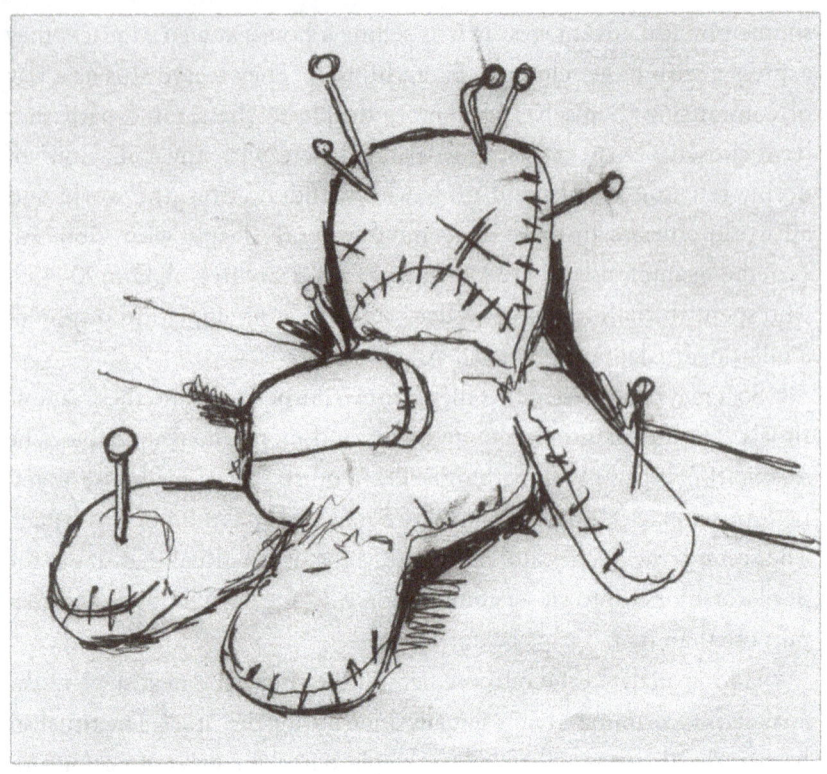

Magical doll or "poppet" used by Satanists to injure or destroy an enemy, or to dispose of what they consider to be a problem.

Satanists are very frequently thought to celebrate a strange reversal of the Catholic Mass, referred to as the Black Mass, but it is highly probable that this ritual is, in fact, only rarely performed. The full Christian Mass, also referred to as the Eucharist, Holy Communion, and as the Holy Sacrament, consists of blessing bread and wine – usually special wafers instead of actual bread – which are then thought of as the Body and Blood of Christ. These are distributed to worshippers by the priest who is celebrating the Mass. For those Christians who believe that an *actual change* takes place in the bread and wine when they are blessed by the priest, the theological term used is *transubstantiation*. For those Christian worshippers who believe that in a very special way Christ *accompanies* the blessed bread and wine, the theological term used is *consubstantiation*. For Satanists following the Black Mass ritual, sacred bread and wine from a Christian Mass are profaned in some way. Their Black Mass then becomes a parody of the Christian Mass.

There is a wide range of ideas among Satanists about *how* the blessed Christian bread and wine can be obtained. In some cases, it is a matter of blatant theft from a Christian Church where sacred bread and wine is known to be stored in case it is needed urgently for a dying believer who hopes to take the Blessed Sacrament before passing over. In other cases, there is a corrupt Christian priest who has made a contract with Satan. This priest will then bring blessed bread and wine to the Black Mass ceremony. In some cases, such a corrupt priest will actually conduct the Black Mass by acting as a satanic priest during that ritual.

It has also been suggested that supposed Christians attending a Catholic Mass would secrete the bread under the tongue and then give it to their Satanist colleagues later. Satanist authors and commentators on the Black Mass tend to disagree about the techniques of profaning the stolen sacred bread and wine. Some accounts describe it as being profaned during acts of satanic sexual magic. Others suggest that it is replaced by profane objects rather than actually being profaned itself. Profane substitutes have been said to include a toad, a turnip, other root vegetable, or pieces of dried flesh.

Some historians have suggested that one possible origin of the Black Mass could be found in a medieval parody of the Mass written in ecclesiastical Latin during the thirteenth century. This was referred to as the Drinkers' and Gamblers' Mass, and was probably intended to draw critical attention to the drinking and gambling of corrupt and dissolute monks. The parody used Bacchus (the god of wine) in place of Deus (God). The work was found in a collection of medieval Latin poetry entitled *Carmina Burana* (Songs from Beuern), which appeared around the year 1230.

In medieval times the ritual of the Mass was not firmly fixed and there were opportunities for priests to add what were referred to as private or secret prayers. Some priests began to offer to celebrate Mass for a fee to meet the needs of their personal clients: obtaining the love of a desirable potential partner, blessing crops and harvests, or dealing with enemies. This was a particularly unpleasant practice: the enemy's name was included in a Mass for the dead and a doll, or poppet, representing the enemy was buried.

Part of the European witch-hunting procedures consisted of accusing those suspected of wizardry, witchcraft, and black magic of perverting the Christian Mass. They were thought to do this in their role as agents of the devil. They were said to be using stolen Christian bread for their own satanic purposes. The notorious textbook for witch-hunters, *Malleus Maleficarum*, gave details of the ways that witches supposedly did this.

For some three hundred years, starting in the sixteenth century, there were reports of the Black Mass being performed by Satanists in France. Catherine de Medici was said to have carried out the ceremony based on the details given in a book by Jean Bodin.

Another exponent of the Black Mass was the notorious poisoner Catherine Montvoisin (1640–80), usually referred to simply as La Voisin. She was deeply implicated in the infamous *affaire des poisons* during the reign of Louis XIV. Her husband was an unsuccessful jeweller and she began to dabble in Satanism and black magic to bring in some extra income. Catherine arranged abortions, acted as a midwife on other occasions, and mixed strange herbal and alchemical medicines, including aphrodisiacs. She also found it lucrative to supply poisons when the price was right. One of her many magician lovers and accomplices was Adam Coeuret, who was also known as Lesage. A corrupt priest named Étienne Guibourg also joined her in these nefarious activities, and the blood of children was used as part of their version of the Black Mass.

One of La Voisin's clients was Olympe Mancini, the Comtesse de Soissons, who wanted Mme de Montespan, the king's mistress, poisoned. The ingredients of some of these unsavoury concoctions included human blood, dust from a burial place, cantharides, iron filings, mole teeth, and toad bones.

La Voisin was convicted of witchcraft and burned alive in a public square in the Fourth Arrondissement of Paris. The square was known as the Place de Grève prior to 1802, the word *grève* meaning a flat area covered with sand or gravel on the shore of an ocean, lake, or river. Since 1802 it has been known as the Place de l'Hotel de Ville. It was a popular site for both public meetings and public executions. Although also deeply involved in La Voisin's unpleasant activities, the renegade priest Guibourg was imprisoned instead of being executed. He died in prison in 1686 at the age of seventy-six.

La Voisin and Étienne Guibourg also performed Black Masses on behalf of Françoise-Athénaïs de Rochechouart de Mortemart, Marquise de

Montespan (1641-1707), better known as Madame de Montespan, who was the most famous mistress of Louis XIV, with whom she had seven children.

When La Voisin and Guibourg performed the ceremony with Montespan, she was lying naked on her back on the altar with her arms outstretched and a black candle in each hand. The chalice was placed on her stomach, and their parody of the Mass proceeded from there.

The infamous Donatien Alphonse François, Marquis de Sade (1740-1814), included references to the Black Mass in many of his writings, and in all probability actually participated in several.

The French author Charles-Marie-Georges Huysmans (1848-1907), who published his works as Joris-Karl Huysmans, wrote on French Satanism in *Là-Bas*, which appeared in 1891. Characters in the book hold long discussions on the history of Satanism in France. One of them then takes part in a Black Mass of the type that Huysmans seemed to think was actually practised in Paris. Although ostensibly a work of fiction, *Là-Bas* went into a wealth of realistic detail about the Black Mass, detail which led many readers to suspect that Huysmans had some special inside knowledge of it. The priest in *Là-Bas*, however, does not actually perform a satanic ritual: he goes into a long argument praising Satan as a god of reason, who is opposed to the restrictive formalism of Christianity. Huysmans' priest in *Là-Bas* seems closer to the writings of the French poet Charles Pierre Baudelaire (1821-67) than to any type of parody or subversion of the Christian Mass.

Jules Michelet (1798-1874), the French historian, wrote *La Sorcière*, retitled *Satanism and Witchcraft* in 1862. Two chapters of this work refer to the Black Mass in an analytical way that enabled Michelet's readers to gain a clearer understanding of what it was.

James George Frazer (1854-1941) was the brilliant Scottish social anthropologist who wrote *The Golden Bough* in 1890. This outstanding study contains details of worldwide magical and religious beliefs. His basic hypothesis was that human belief went through three distinct stages: magic, religion, and science. Frazer included a detailed description of the Mass of Saint Sécaire – a type of Black Mass, which he had discovered in *Quatorze Superstitions Populaires de la Gascogne*, published in 1883. This book (Fourteen Popular Superstitions of Gascony) had been written by Jean-François Bladé (1827-1900), a French historian and folklore expert.

The Mass of Saint Sécaire can be regarded as a parody of the traditional Roman Catholic Mass. It was distinguished from other versions of the Black Mass because it was allegedly used as a secret means of killing when someone was looking for vengeance.

The Mass of Saint Sécaire had to be performed by a corrupt priest and his sex partner in a ruined or abandoned church. The ceremony needed to begin exactly on the stroke of eleven o'clock at night, and had to be finished precisely on the final stroke of midnight. The corrupt priest recited the Christian Mass backward and used wafers that were black and triangular in shape as distinct from the circular white wafers of the traditional Christian Eucharist. Instead of the wine used at a proper Christian Mass, the corrupt priest drank water that had been drawn from a well containing the body of an unbaptized infant. The celebrant would make the sign of the cross on the ground using his left foot. As soon as the ceremony was complete, the renegade priest would whisper the name of the victim against whom the Mass of Saint Sécaire was being directed. It was believed that he, or she, would then die without any apparent cause, and that a post-mortem examination of the victim's corpse would reveal no clues.

Other literature concerning the nature of the Black Mass came from the sinister pen of Aleister Crowley (1875–1947). He wrote a short story about the Mass of Saint Sécaire in his series based upon Frazer's *Golden Bough*, entitled *Golden Twigs*. This was first published in 1918 in *The International* then appeared in a later publication in 1988.

Another source of information on various aspects of Satanist ceremonies and the Black Mass was Augustus Montague Summers (1880–1948). In his book on the subject, *The History of Witchcraft and Demonology*, Chapter IV, The Sabbat, he uses many quotations from Latin and French texts.

As far as can be ascertained from these and other sources, the Black Mass can be divided into half a dozen separate sections. The first is categorized as the *introit*, which is an introduction to the ceremony that is to follow. The priest talks to his followers and assistants about the purpose of the Black Mass and what the subsequent stages will involve. There are parts of this introit that are very similar to the introduction to the normal Christian Mass, but all the dedications are changed, and the names Satan, Lucifer, Beelzebub, or simply "the devil" are substituted for those of God and Christ. During this introit the woman who will serve as the altar is stripped and placed on her back, with a black candle in each hand. The priest's assistants, known as acolytes, then light the candles and the censers (incense burners). This can be regarded as the end of the introit.

The second stage is a preparation for the ceremony that is to follow. Accompanied by two assistants – one boy and one girl – the priest approaches the girl serving as the altar and performs brief introductory sexual acts with her. The remainder of this preparation stage involves the ritual touching of the stolen sacramental wafer, the censers, the chalice, and the candles that will be part of the later ceremony. The wafer may not actually have been stolen from a church or tabernacle, but "consecrated" in advance by the corrupt priest. Satanist groups differ in their opinions of whether a wafer supposedly consecrated by a renegade priest can actually be regarded as consecrated at all. They prefer to steal genuinely consecrated wafers from a church where they have been consecrated by an authentic and sincere priest.

Just as the consecrated wafers are a vital part of the Black Mass, so too is the wine. Tarragona, in eastern Spain, produces a delicious, rich red wine that is greatly favoured for Christian Masses. It is often selected by Satanists for Black Masses, as well, but they will often contaminate it before the mass with noxious, hallucinogenic substances.

Experts on the Black Mass maintain that the satanic chalice cannot be made of gold. Just as silver is traditionally fatal for vampires and werewolves, so gold is said to be too pure and holy to become a usable part of a satanic Black Mass.

The chalice is fitted with a paten (a thin, circular plate) and a veil, both decorated with satanic symbols. Other accessories include a thurible (or censer) and an incense boat, charcoal, and methylated spirit or similar fuel. Just as the red wine of Tarragona is fouled when used at a Black Mass, the incense is also contaminated. Typical Black Mass incense is reported to contain asphalt or tar, myrrh, and various toxic herbs such as henbane (*Hyoscyamus niger*), thornapple (*Datura stramonium*), and deadly nightshade (*Atropa belladonna*). In Greek mythology, Atropos was the third of the Fates – the one who cut the thread when a life ended.

Another important accessory for the Black Mass is an image of Satan, displayed prominently in the location of the ceremony. The particular type of image depends upon which group of Satanists are performing the ritual. Luciferans tend to envisage Lucifer as an attractive young man – the morning and evening star, a male equivalent of the sex-goddess, Venus. Other groups might select the goat image, or a hybrid form like Pan.

A bell is considered an essential piece of ritual equipment, and is duly rung at high points in the ceremony. In some versions of the ritual, an aspergillus (a form of toxic fungus) of an obviously suggestive shape is also involved, as well as a small cauldron.

Robes vary from one sect of Satanists to another. Some favour elaborately embroidered priestly vestments that would grace the staff of the most ornate cathedral; others prefer simple, smock-like garments that can be swiftly and easily discarded when the orgiastic part of the ceremony begins.

Satanists at a Black Mass.

The actual words of a satanic Black Mass liturgy also differ from one sect to another. The general pattern, translated into English, broadly follows this outline, with V representing the verse, words spoken by the priest, and the R the worshippers' response:

> **V: In the Name of the great god Satan we will enter this altar of the Lord of Hell.**
> R: *He gives us joy.*
> **V: Our Infernal Lord will grant us his help.**
> R: *He is the ruler of the Earth.*
> **V: The Earth is yours, Lord Lucifer. Aid me against my enemies, for I am your true servant. Preserve and protect me from those who persecute me.**
> R: *Deliver us from all who hate us without cause.*
> **V: Come to us, Lord Satan, and give us new life.**
> R: *We are your people and you will make us glad.*
> **V: Show us your great power, Lord Satan.**
> R: *Give us your generous gifts to enjoy.*
> **V: Hear us, mighty Satan. Hear us, great Lucifer.**
> R: *Let our voices reach you.*
> **V: May the Lord of Hell be with you.**
> R: *And also with you.*
> **V: All power and glory to Satan, Lucifer, Beelzebub, and Asmodeus.**
> R: *We praise and honour the Lords of Earth and Hell.*

The third section of the Black Mass is referred to as the *offertory*. The wafers and wine are shown to the congregation, and the priest then censes the naked female altar and the table or platform on which she has been placed. The celebrant then raises the wine and wafer and offers them to Satan. He then invites Satan to come and bless the participants. His assistants then bring him the thurible and the incense, which he sprinkles on the glowing charcoal.

> **V: May this incense rise to you and please you, Lord of Hell.**
> R: *May your gifts descend upon us.*

The celebrant then censes the picture of Satan, and the naked girl who constitutes the altar. If there is sufficient space, he walks all around her as he does the censing.

> **V: The Lord of Hell be with you.**
> **R:** *And also with you.*
> **V: Lift up your hearts.**
> **R:** *We lift our hearts to the Lord of Hell.*
> **V: Let us give thanks to our Infernal Lord.**
> **R:** *It is meet and right to do so.*
> **V: It is truly meet and right that we should praise and thank him at all times and in every place.**

The celebrant then bows to the picture of Satan and rings the bell three times (in other versions, the bell is rung either seven or nine times).

> **V: All hail to you, Lord of Power, ruler of Earth and Hell. All praise and glory to you, our master.**

The fourth section of the Black Mass is known as the canon, and it is in this section that the ceremony begins to plumb the depths of depravity in ways that involve the congregation. The celebrant makes sexual contact with the girl acting as the altar, and the congregation start to remove their clothes in preparation for the traditional orgy that follows. Aspersion with the urine of an acolyte is also involved.

In the fifth section of the Black Mass, referred to as the consecration, further sexual activity takes place between the celebrant and the girl serving as the altar.

Various blasphemous parodies of the Christian Mass are uttered by the celebrant and the congregation, who are by now heavily under the influence of the hallucinatory toxins in the wine and the incense to which they have been exposed.

The bell is then rung again three, seven, or nine times to usher in the sixth and final stage, known to Satanists as the repudiation. This title suggests that all traditional morality and ethics are repudiated. This terminal section can best be described as a situation in which all hell breaks loose! The priest, the girl, the acolytes, and all the congregation participate in an uninhibited orgy fuelled by drugs and alcohol and often, reportedly, involving incest.

In addition to the features of the Black Mass outlined above, there are many other forms of satanic ceremony, including the initiation rites for witches and wizards. These exist in several forms, just as the Black Mass does. There are three levels of initiation that are traditionally observed. They are known as the First, Second, and Third Degrees – broadly corresponding to the academic levels of Bachelor, Master, and Doctor. The lowest of the three degrees is referred to as Witch or Priest of Lucifer, Satan, or of the great goddess – possibly Astarte. The second degree is called Magus or, in the case of a female candidate, Witch Queen. The highest of the three degrees is called High Priest or High Priestess.

A candidate for the First Degree is led into the so-called circle of power, naked and blindfolded, with hands fastened behind the back. Ceremonial kissing in different positions takes place; the candidate is then ceremonially whipped and swears an oath of secrecy. The oath contains the words, "of my own free will ... I most solemnly vow that I will always keep secret ... and never reveal the mysteries of the magic art except to an authorized person ... within a circle of power ... and that the secrets of the art shall never be denied to such a one...."

This ostensible oath of secrecy would seem to be more fragile than eggshells as the so-called secrets of the art have been recorded in books, broadcast on radio and TV, and appeared in the press and other media from time to time.

After taking the oath, various items of "magical equipment" are given to the candidate, and their uses explained. One of these tools is referred to as the *athame*, a knife with a black hilt. Early references to the *athame* were found in *Clavicula Salomonis: The Key of Solomon*, or *Mafteah Shelomoh* in Hebrew. This is a grimoire dating back to the fourteenth century and attributed to King Solomon the Wise. The initiate is told that the *athame* will enable him to dominate evil spirits, jinn, and demons, and to persuade angels and good spirits to help and protect him. At the conclusion of this First Degree service, the initiate is told that he is now a full-fledged priest of Lucifer and of the great goddess.

The Second Degree is similar to the first, but the scourging (whipping) now becomes a two-way process and the candidate scourges the initiator in return for the blows that he or she receives. The next stage is to read the legend of the goddess — a modified version of the myth of Persephone, Hades, Demeter, and the pomegranate seeds. In some versions of the Second Degree ceremony this story is acted out rather than read.

Another myth is allegedly told on some occasions instead of the Demeter and Persephone story. This alternative rendering is based on the very old Canaanite myth of a character called Shaher, the morning star (really the planet Venus as seen in the morning) and his twin brother, Shalem, the evening star (also the planet Venus, but as seen in the evening). There is a strong possibility that Shaher and Shalem can be identified with Castor and Pollux of the later Greek legend. The second degree initiate is taught to understand light and darkness, summer and winter, from either or both of these legends. After listening to the stories, the candidate is told that life contains three great events — love, death, and resurrection in a new body — but that magic is supreme over all of these. Finally, the initiate is taken around the circle of power and proclaimed a new Magus or Witch Queen.

The Third Degree focuses on ritualized sexual activity in which the *athame* is dipped into a container of wine. The onlookers are told that these objects represent the sexes — the knife being male and the cup of wine female. As soon as this has been done, the graduate is declared to be a High Priest or Priestess, a position holding great power in the world of Satanism, witchcraft, wizardry, and magic.

Another very unusual and interesting ritual, known as the Star Energy Spell, is known to have taken place at some magical conventions and Satanists' meetings. It is performed outside on clear nights when stars are visible. Believers in these spells regard the stars and planets as having very different types of energy. Venus clearly indicates a source of energy for magicians and Satanists performing sex spells. Polaris and Caput Algol, the Gorgon's Head, located in Taurus, are both regarded as very dangerous and capable of causing insanity in those who is use them!

The spell begins when the users relax and go into a trance-like state. They then chant the name of the star that they are planning to use as an energy source. After a few minutes the group begins to think that they can actually feel the energy radiating from the star into them. Each member of the group then begins to concentrate on his or her own aura, and endeavours to charge it with stellar energy until they feel that it is actually glowing. In the next stage, the participants try to feel the Earth's energy through the magician's feet. Once they feel this has been accomplished, the magician visualizes a line of energy roughly half a metre wide extending from him up to the chosen star. The group members then begin to breathe in the stellar energy, which is a different colour depending on which star or planet is being used. The planet Venus sends out green energy thought to produce sexual love and wealth; yellow energy is thought to enhance intellect and problem-solving abilities; and orange energy gives extra creativity. Red energy from the planet Mars is believed to promote violent, aggressive power, whereas stars or planets that deliver blue energy convey calmness, peace, and spirituality.

In these very different ways, Satanists and magicians perform various rituals ranging from the Black Mass to an attempt to obtain magical stellar energy. An analysis of these examples sheds a great deal of cautionary light on the extent of human credulity and the darkest types of human motivation, together with the unpleasant extremes into which human beings can sink.

SATANIC SEX MAGIC

It has become commonplace for sensational accusations regarding sexuality to be levelled at Satanists, pagans, witches, and wizards. Media headlines relating to satanic sexuality or black magic and sexuality are likely to persuade a few additional readers to buy the tabloid concerned.

Looked at from another perspective, however, the question might be raised as to whether the church's insistence on restricting sexual activity to marriage, and in some cases prohibiting contraception, has helped to create a social atmosphere in which a great many people are sexually frustrated.

Paganism, and the Old Religion of pre-Christian times, needs to be separated from later witchcraft, black magic, and Satanism. Pagans believed, and still believe, that as their gods saw fit to provide humans with the means to enjoy sex, there is no logical reason why they shouldn't do so at every opportunity.

Formal, traditional Christianity by contrast has advocated celibacy, virginity and sexual abstinence of one type or another. Even though St. Paul argued in One Corinthians 7:9 that as a last resort it was better to marry than to burn with passion, he was scarcely expressing enthusiasm for sex!

Another major factor in the sociology of sex can be traced to a favoured advertising technique in which whatever good or service is being pitched — hairstyling, tanning, brands of alcohol, or sports cars — the implication is that buying the product or using the service will attract an unlimited supply of sexually enthusiastic partners.

Pagans, witches, wizards, and Satanists in the twenty-first century seem to advocate the enjoyment of uninhibited sexual activity in much less subtle ways than advertisers imply.

Whereas Christian theologians seem to have had a preference for excluding sex from religious observance, the pre-Christian pagans found sex to be an integral part of their fertility cults.

It has been suggested that *Malleus Maleficarum* — written by Heinrich Kramer in 1486 and dubiously associated with Jacob Sprenger as co-author to lend it some respectability and academic authority — was more of a treatise on misogyny than on witchcraft. Any Freudian psychoanalyst would have been highly suspicious of Kramer's mindset and motives. His apparent fear of sex and aversion to women could have been his prime motivators rather than any genuine interest in preventing the alleged ill effects of black magic. Although at one time an inquisitor, Kramer was denounced by the Inquisition in 1490, which reveals a great deal about this curious man and his motives.

Kramer's misogyny becomes apparent when the early section of *Malleus Maleficarum* suggests that women are more likely to become witches than men are. He asserts that women have numerous weaknesses that make them vulnerable to demonic influences. In Kramer's opinion, their Christian faith is weaker and their carnal desires are much stronger than those of men. Even the Latin title of Kramer's book is feminized grammatically: *Maleficorum* with an *o* is the masculine form, but *Maleficarum* with an *a* is the feminine form that Kramer selected.

Despite Kramer's curious ideas in *Malleus Maleficarum*, however, the links between Satanism, black magic, witchcraft, and sexuality are powerful and prominent.

Human sexuality needs to be defined and understood in order to analyze the related factors within Satanism and black magic. Human sexuality can be seen as the way in which people experience the erotic as such, and how they express themselves as sexual entities. There are three main categories of human sexuality: emotional, physical, and biological.

The main driving force behind the whole of sexuality is the desire for sexual pleasure. The emotional aspects of sexuality are the feelings that are part of the sexual act itself, and these emotions are among the most powerful that a human being experiences. These emotions are also inseparable from various social bonds.

The physical dimensions of sexuality can be medical at one extreme, involving contraception, sexually transmitted diseases, and the complications of pregnancy, and physiological at the other end of the scale, where copulative techniques, various positions, and types of sexual contact are considered.

Sexuality can be categorized biologically as the means of procreation of the species along with the deep, instinctive drive to reproduce.

Human sexuality can become extremely complicated by culture and society. There are philosophical and theological aspects, as well as legal and political ones. There are deep questions of morality, ethics, religion, and spirituality. This is where the directness of Satanism often makes its appeal as an apparent cutting of the Gordian knot of sexual restrictions and taboos. "Do what thou wilt is the whole of the law," can seem attractive to those who are on the lookout to increase their sexual activities.

The endless nature versus nurture debate is as relevant for human sexuality as for almost all other aspects of human life and behaviour. There is a great deal more to the sexual attitudes that people *develop* than the simple instincts with which they are *born*. The ways that individuals identify themselves, and then recognize their place in society, have extremely strong sexual aspects that are learned as well as innate. Human sexual activity is the product of intellectual activity as well as hormonal activity. It depends to a significant extent on where and when a person was brought up and the social influences in place during that time.

There are medical experts who argue that regular sexual activity has a great many beneficial effects on health: it reduces stress; it increases the body's production of immunoglobulin (an antibody that plays an essential role in immunity); it reduces the risk of heart attack; it helps produce deep, sound sleep; and it greatly reduces the risk of prostate cancer in men.

Human sexuality is also very much a part of social life, where it influences the social norms and mores and is in turn influenced by them. In much the same way, sexuality has a powerful influence on the mass media, and is influenced by it.

Any complete and proper understanding of sex and Satanism, and the involvement of sex in witchcraft and black magic involves an examination of the psychology of sex. Sigmund Freud (1856-1939) pioneered the psychoanalytical approach to it, and his major theories include the concept of erogenous zones, psychosexual development, and the Oedipus complex. In 1913, Carl Jung (1875-1961) formulated his Electra complex, the antithesis of Freud's latter theory.

The school of psychologists referred to as Behaviourists included John B. Watson (1878-58) and B.F. Skinner (1904-90), who characteristically examined actions and their consequences — essentially, cause and effect. Their contribution to sexual psychology was to examine sexual activity that may have taken place in an individual's past for which they had been punished, or from which he or she suffered some unpleasant consequence. The Behaviourist would then look to see whether that episode had given the person a negative attitude toward sexual activity.

Another interesting and important aspect of the analysis of human sexuality and its link with Satanism and witchcraft is described as gender identity. There is the individual's own innate, instinctive sense of gender identity, and then there is the broader question of the social construction of gender identity.

Human sexuality, motivated by pleasure-seeking, involves the search for a partner or partners with whom the individual can interact sexually to achieve orgasm.

Sexual attraction is a vital ingredient in the search for a prospective partner. Which qualities does a person regard as attractive in another person? This varies widely depending upon the person's sexual orientation — and there are certain broad categories here in connection with sex, Satanism, and witchcraft. There are individuals who seek to dominate; others enjoy being dominated.

Sadists — and there are likely a number of these among Satanists and inquisitors — enjoy inflicting pain, suffering, and humiliation.

Masochists — again prevalent among Satanists and black magicians — achieve their sexual excitement from having pain inflicted on them. Voyeurs obtain sexual excitement from watching sexual activity. Fetishists can be attracted by shoes, jewellery, or tattoos, for example. Voyeurism and fetishism are both frequently encountered in satanic sexual situations.

Another aspect of human sexuality is the desire to attract others for the purpose of sexual activity, and there is a large element of this in satanic sexual interactions. A witches' coven or a group of Satanists may endeavour to attract new members to share their sexual activities.

One of the major attractions of sex in the context of Satanism, witchcraft, and black magic is its freedom from the ethical and moral codes that try to govern and control sex in other social contexts. All the major religions have their particular moral and ethical codes governing sexual behaviour, encompassing with whom, where, and when it may take place.

Very often, however, human sexual activity contravenes these norms and mores, and the rules laid down by various religious bodies. Most religions, for example, disapprove of sexual activities outside marriage — but human sexual desire is frequently so strong that such extramarital sexual activities still take place in spite of religious prohibition.

Any full and proper understanding of sexual magic and the sexual rituals that form part of Satanism begins with the idea of sex as a powerful force. Sexual magic and sexual rituals in Satanism seek to use that force, to trap the natural energy it contains, and to redirect it to serve their own ends. Undeniably, there are elements of voyeurism, fetishism, rape, sadomasochism, and sexual torture present in sexual magic and satanic sexual rituals, but there are other elements, as well. Sex in these contexts is not seen by the magician or the Satanist as an end in itself — although for some participants it probably is. The Satanist and the black magician are both trying to use sex as an energy source — as well as something that they simply enjoy doing.

Some groups of Satanists emphasize sex in their rituals and almost invariably end a ceremony with an orgy. Other groups try to use sex at a deeper level, as a mechanism for exploring the depth of an individual's personality. They argue that as sex is such an important part of a human life, if a person can understand and develop his or her sexuality to its fullest extent, the personality will be enriched and developed, and enabled to achieve greater success in every field. These groups teach their members to experiment freely with their sexuality until they find out what gives them the greatest pleasure.

The more sophisticated teachers of Satanism in groups who hold this developmental view of sexuality persuade their followers that sex is the quickest route to the human subconscious, and that once the subconscious has been reached, magic may more easily and effectively be performed. This, again, comes close to the idea that if and when magic works, it is not the ingredients in the cauldron that do anything, nor is it the talisman or amulet. The real power is in the mind of the magician. Paracelsus (1493-1541), the great Renaissance physician, botanist, occultist, alchemist, and astrologer, was absolutely right when he wrote: "*Thoughts* create a new heaven, a new firmament, a new source of energy, from which new arts flow."

Instructions for performing one particular magical rite vary, but it is generally recommend that a priest and priestess, both properly initiated into their black magic sect, seek out an isolated hilltop or mountain peak and remove their clothing. Their sacred robes should be folded in accordance with a prescribed pattern and laid together. Sounds are an important part of this version of the ritual. The words may vary from one cult to another, but can be said a syllable at a time as follows: *Nee-thrar-cthun-aye-att-arz-oth*. It is not only these sounds themselves that the magicians and Satanists regard as sounds of power, but the length of time relative to the other syllables for which each is sounded. A minimum of thirty seconds each is recommended. The participants believe that these noises can stimulate the mind, and, more or less as Paracelsus taught, can energize their thoughts very effectively.

While the priest is sounding out the necessary syllables, the priestess holds a crystal in front of his mouth. Almost any crystal of any shape and material is alleged to work, but some experts advocate using quartz — if possible, quartz with a four-sided shape. It has been found that a quartz tetrahedron vibrates more effectively than crystals of other materials and shapes.

Once the crystal is vibrating to the satisfaction of both the priest and priestess, further sexual activity takes place between them. She imagines that she can see a cosmic portal in the stars above them, from which raw chaotic energy that they can use in their magic is flowing down to the Earth beside them.

Another way of performing the ritual, described as the Chthonic Method, requires satanic worshippers in addition to the priest and priestess. There should be a minimum of fourteen — seven men and seven women — to participate in the orgy once the Chthonic Rite is completed. The setting now should be a deep valley with a stream running through it, or better still, a large cavern with water in it. The crystal will be included in the ceremony as before.

Different, more elaborate words are chanted. These vary from one group to another but include the syllables *Binn-ann-ath-ga-waf-amm*. The worshippers then call on Satan, Lucifer, Beelzebub, and other demons to appear and commune with them. In some extreme rituals, members of certain sects believe that the energy from this Chthonic Ritual endows the

Priest and priestess.

priest or priestess with the power of the antichrist and that such a being would be able to perform very powerful magic indeed!

The worshippers believe that by participating in an orgy at the end of their Chthonic Ritual, they are overcoming what they consider to be the negative influences of Christianity and the other major religions that put limits on sexual behaviour. They consider that the universal prohibitions and regulations that limit human sexuality have had a damaging effect on the energy that nature intends should be released by widespread sexual activity. Some sects who perform the Chthonic Ritual believe that the energy they have released during the orgy can be stored in their quartz tetrahedron and buried safely in the ground until it is required for further black magic.

Another satanic ritual involving sexual magic is referred to as Creating the Circle. It is meant to create a circle either for protection or to entrap dark spirits.

The priest and priestess begin by removing their robes and then placing four candles at the four cardinal points. In the centre, the satanic altar can be a rock or tree stump. There is no reason why a table cannot be used, but most magicians prefer a natural altar as the centre. The magical tools for the ceremony consist of an *athame*, a wand, a sword, a small cauldron, incense, some crystals — preferably quartz — and a selection of herbs and spices. Two extra candles are placed on the altar so that there are six candles in all. These are then lit.

Spells and sexuality.

Appropriate satanic music is started — drums and cymbals that are beaten rhythmically by the congregation assisting the priest and priestess, who then kneel beside the altar, facing east. The cauldron is filled with water and placed on the altar. The priestess purifies the water with a short prayer that asks the spirits to cleanse the water. She uses the names of Lucifer and Beelzebub, although some ritual groups may invoke other powerful members of the demonic hierarchy, including Astarte and Lilith. The priest then inserts his *athame* into the cauldron of purified water as a sexual symbol, just as the cauldron of water itself symbolizes the priestess. He drops the quartz crystal into the water, and retrieves it with his left hand. It is then dried on the altar cloth and placed carefully among the herbs and spices. These are now lifted onto the altar with the quartz crystal.

The priestess then moves away, and the priest, using the sword, draws a circle incorporating the four candles that mark the cardinal points. As he does this he envisages power flowing like lightning from the point of the sword into the Earth. He blesses the circle that he has drawn and declares it to be a protected realm, so that any demons or spirits that are summoned within it cannot escape, and will be unable to harm the worshippers. He then leaves the circle, and returns with the priestess, whom he greets with a series of kisses. She then leaves the circle and returns with one of the men, who takes off his robes. She kisses him, and he then leaves the circle to fetch one of the women from outside. She takes off her robes. He kisses her. She then leaves the circle and returns with a man. The ritual continues in this way until all the coven is inside the circle. The cauldron of purified water is passed from one worshipper to another. A male sprinkles a female alternately. The priest and priestess are anointed last. The ceremony is then concluded with general sexual activity among the coven members.

One of the most unpleasant spells used by witches, wizards, black magicians, and Satanists — especially in the United States — is the preparation of *kufwa* dust. This name comes from the Kikongo language, the Bantu language spoken by the Bakongo people from the Democratic Republic of the Congo. It was the language spoken by many slaves in the eighteenth and nineteenth centuries, which is how it made its way to the United States, Haiti, Cuba, and Brazil. Kufwa dust is used by black magicians to bring death and disaster down upon their enemies.

Because of the general belief in black magic circles that sexual activity releases energy and so increases the power of the spell — in this case the malevolent potency of the fatal kufwa dust — sexual activity frequently accompanies the mixing of the unsavoury ingredients: graveyard soil, the skin of rattlesnakes, powdered toxic herbs such as henbane, and sulphur powder. The Satanist, witch, or wizard directing the power of the *kufwa* powder against an enemy will take up one of the enemy's footprints from soft soil and mix it with the kufwa dust. This mixture is then placed inside a magic bottle (of green or black glass) and hidden in the bowl of a hollow tree, as close to the victim's house as possible.

Just as sexuality is a major motif in the whole of human life, both individually and socially, so it permeates magic and Satanism. It attracts voyeurs and there are elements of sadomasochism in it. There is also a dark and sinister sense in which the torturers working for the Inquisition found misogynistic sadistic sexual pleasures in abusing and torturing their female victims.

The Seventy-Two Solomonic Demons

According to legend, the great and wise King Solomon (*circa* B.C. 1000–930) possessed a very powerful magic ring bearing the seal of Solomon and giving him power over demons. In some versions of the legend of Solomon's power over the demons, this magic ring was called the Ring of Aandaleeb. Using its great power, Solomon captured seventy-two powerful demons and used them to carry out various projects for him. They are well-known to Satanists, black magicians, wizards, and witches. Each has a different name and a different range of powers and attributes.

Agares appears in the form of a handsome older man. He carries a goshawk on his right wrist while riding a crocodile, which ambles along at a steady pace. He has the power to freeze runners in their tracks and to bring runaway slaves to their lawful masters. He is a brilliant linguist and teaches languages to his worshippers and supporters. His powers include the ability to bring down the mighty from their exalted positions — whether they are high-ranking demons or high-ranking humans. He also has the power to cause earthquakes. Those who can secure his services — as Solomon did, in legend — are well-guarded because Agares drives away the enemies of those he serves.

Aini is a very formidable-looking demon. Although he has a strong male human body, it is surmounted by three heads: a serpent, a cat, and a human male with stars embellishing his forehead. He rides on a toxic snake and carries a blazing torch with which he sets fire to forests and houses. Aini gives the gift of subtle cunning to his followers. He will also, if commanded and controlled properly, provide secret information regarding private, closely-hidden matters.

Allocen appears in the form of a cavalryman. He has the face of a lion, but is very red all over. His voice is hoarse, very loud and unpleasant. He has a great knowledge of science — as many of the demons have — and leaves a useful familiar spirit with his worshippers to assist them.

Amduscias looks like a unicorn, but can assume human shape. He has abnormal powers over music and many types of musical instruments. He has the power to uproot trees and make them fall.

Amon has the head of a snake mounted on a huge wolf's body. He can spit flame like a dragon, and can even take on the appearance of a human being, but when he does so his wolf's teeth remain. He is able to see the past, the present, and the future simultaneously — although the future he sees remains as a series of *probabilities*: there are no pre-ordained *certainties*. He can be called upon to bring sexually desired partners to those he serves, and can cause his master's enemies to become friends and allies instead.

Amy is a very powerful demon who arrives first as a great ball of flame. Soon afterward, he takes on the appearance of a man. He can give knowledge of stars, moons, and planets, and is well-versed in other sciences also. Under the control of a powerful magician, he can lead people to hidden treasures of great value.

Andras has the body of an angel, but the head of a black wolf. He carries a flashing blade and is very dangerous. He enjoys killing, and must be kept strictly under control. His presence causes quarrels and disputes.

Andrealphus is a bird-like demon, who can sometimes appear as a beautiful peacock or other exotic bird. Those who summon and try to control him must be particularly careful because he has the power to turn human beings into birds. He has power over measurements and shapes, and is an expert in all branches of geometry, including the geometry of the heavens, and the positions of the stars in their constellations.

Andromalius is in human form and carries a snake in one hand. A controlling magician can use Andromalius's power to recover stolen property and apprehend a thief. This demon is able to expose trickery, deceit, and crime. Like several others of his kind, he can lead the way to hidden treasures.

Asmoday is a very high-ranking spirit, a veritable king among demons. He has three heads: one human, one of a ram, and another resembling a bull. His powerful body ends with a long tail like the body of a serpent. He can spit fire and his feet are curiously webbed like those of a great water bird. He rides a huge dragon and carries a venomous lance. In his presence, it is part of the ritual that the magician removes his hat. He is the master of numerology and arithmetic, and can teach all manner of crafts and skills. His greatest gift to those who can control him is the power of invisibility. Like many other demons, he can guide those who master him to the site of hidden treasure.

Astaroth has the appearance of a beautiful, angelic being, which contrasts sharply with the dragon on which he rides. In his right hand he holds a deadly poisonous snake. Any magician seeking to use his powers needs to avoid Astaroth's reeking breath, which carries the stench of death and decay. Astaroth has great knowledge of all sciences, as well as every event in history. He denies that he is one of the fallen angels — although he certainly is! Any magician using his services needs the protection of a magical silver ring. To make contact with him even more hazardous, Astaroth has the power to change into the semblance of a very beautiful and seductive demoness. The reeking breath is transformed into a delicious fragrance, like perfume, and the magician is in danger of being lured out of the protected circle.

Baal can give the gift of wisdom when he is properly controlled and subdued. He also has the gift of invisibility. He has a hoarse voice and can appear with the head of a toad, the head of a cat, or the head of a man. Disconcertingly, he can also appear with all three heads simultaneously.

Balam also has three heads: bull, ram, and human. All three are present all the time. He has a long, snaky tail and eyes like lasers. He can give the gift of sharp wits to any who are powerful enough to command him — but it is far from easy to control him. He is also able to give invisibility. He carries a goshawk on his wrist and rides a giant bear.

Barbatos appears when the sun is in Sagittarius. He knows all the sciences and teaches them to those who can subdue him and keep him under control. Another of his skills is the finding of hidden treasure. His linguistic gifts extend to the languages of animals and birds.

Bathin is a demon that appears in the form of a powerful man, but drags his serpentine tail behind him when he walks. On most occasions, however, he rides a light-coloured horse. He is an expert on herbs and their properties as well as on gems and precious stones such as rubies and emeralds. His gifts to those who can subdue and command him are swift transport from one part of the Earth to another. Distance is no object to Bathin.

Beleth is a particularly terrible and powerful demon who is very hard to control. He must be kept carefully within a triangle or circle to prevent him from harming the magician or any of the assembled company who have summoned him. He can be commanded by the use of a hazel twig, which must be kept pointed to the southeast, and the summoning magician needs to wear a silver ring on his left hand. Beleth rides a pale horse and is surrounded by skilled musicians. He can provide the magician with an attractive and enthusiastic sex partner.

Belial in some hierarchies is placed second only to Lucifer. In the mythology of the demons, he was created next after Lucifer. He appears in his original angelic guise, and is extremely beautiful. His voice is as melodic and gentle as his physical appearance, which gives him dangerous powers to deceive. He arrives in a fiery chariot that moves gracefully over land or water. His gifts to those who control him are political rank, fame, and wealth, but he demands sacrifices and offerings or he will not perform.

Berith has many powers, but he is a notorious liar and is extremely treacherous and deceitful. The magician attempting to control him needs a silver ring. Berith resembles a soldier in a red uniform when he appears, and he has the power of turning base metals into gold. He will also provide answers to difficult questions and foretell the future.

Bifrons is a monster that appears in a revolting form, but can assume human shape when ordered to do so by the magician who is controlling him. He is an expert astrologer, and knows a great deal of arithmetic and geometry. He understands all types of wood and timber and is expert with precious stones, gems, and jewels. One of his stranger and darker powers is his control over corpses. He can alter their appearance and bury them in different places. Then he creates phantom candles — corpse candles — and places them over graves.

Botis usually appears in the form of a toxic snake when summoned. He can, however, transform into a humanoid entity with large horns and fangs. He carries a flashing blade and will answer questions about past, present, and future possibilities.

Buer is a particularly valuable and useful demon, and not particularly difficult to summon and control. Once the magician has subdued him, Buer will heal diseases of every kind. He also teaches the properties of healing herbs, and is an expert philosopher and logician.

Bune arrives in the form of a dragon when summoned. The beast has three distinct heads: a man, a savage griffin, and a ferocious hound. He is very powerful and not easy to command or control, but once subdued he bestows wisdom upon his controller and answers difficult questions truthfully. He can also bestow great wealth on those who command him. Although his voice is not unpleasant, he uses it in a sinister way to order demons to cluster around graves and tombs, and he also has the power to alter corpses and move them about.

Caim, rather surprisingly, appears in the guise of a thrush. He then transforms himself into a man carrying a sharp sword. He scatters burning ashes around him. When properly controlled and subdued, his gifts include helping men to understand birdsong and the language of dogs and cattle. He also teaches men to understand the language of rippling water. When forced to answer questions, he speaks truthfully.

Cimeries, when summoned, appears as a soldier astride a huge black war-horse. He is a territorial demon who controls parts of the African continent. When controlled properly, he will teach grammar, rhetoric, and logic and he can help his controller to locate lost objects and buried treasure. He can also make his followers look like soldiers.

Dantalian has many human faces, some male and some female. He carries a book of magic in his right hand, and teaches those who control him not only the arts but the sciences, as well. He can read human minds and persuade people to change their ideas. He has spells that provide his controllers with attractive and willing sex partners.

Multi-faced entity.

Decarabia is a demon who appears as a star inside a magic pentacle, but when controlled and commanded to do so he will appear in human form. He teaches his controllers the use of herbs, and shows the magician how to control birds in flight. These can be transformed into useful familiars should the magician so wish.

Eligor, when summoned, arrives in the guise of a knight on horseback, complete with lance and sceptre. When properly controlled, he can be used by an evil magician to cause wars and conflicts, and to provide attractive, enthusiastic sex partners for the wizard and his companions.

Flauros, when called, appears as a dangerous, aggressive leopard. His controller, however, can order him to assume human form instead, once he has been properly subdued. Even in human form, however, he has blazing eyes and an aggressive expression on his face. He will readily destroy the wizard's enemies while he is under full control, and, perhaps rather strangely, he will not allow other demons or evil spirits to approach his controller and try to tempt him.

Focalor is a water demon who appears in the form of a winged man. His powers extend over the wind and the sea and he delights in sinking ships and drowning passengers and crew. However, once he is fully under the control of his summoner, he will refrain from damaging ships and people.

Forneus is another sea demon, but despite his frightening, monstrous appearance, he is almost benevolent when fully under the magician's control. He can be ordered to reconcile men who were once enemies, and he teaches languages, arts, and the sciences.

Furcas appears as a malevolent-looking old man, with a long white beard, and silver hair. He rides a horse and carries a lethal spear. Once properly controlled and subdued, he can be forced to teach pyromancy, chiromancy, philosophy, logic, rhetoric, and the magic of the stars in their courses.

Furfur appears as a stag with a long, fiery tail. He is very reluctant to speak to the wizard who is controlling him, and has to be forced to do so while pinned within the magic circle or triangle. He changes into an angelic form before speaking and has a number of striking qualities. He can create thunder, lightning, and storm winds, and can enhance the sexual attraction between lovers.

Gaap appears in human form when the sun is among the southern signs of the zodiac, and is always accompanied by four demon kings. Once placed under proper control, Gaap can stimulate love, fear, and hatred, and can also cause unconsciousness. He can arrange almost instantaneous transport, and can free familiars from other magicians should his controller order him to do so. Within the circle or triangle, he will give truthful answers. If he speaks from outside it, he lies.

Gamygyn appears initially in the form of a pony, a donkey, or a small horse, but puts on human shape almost immediately. His main function is to contact the spirits of the dead, especially the spirits of those who have been drowned at sea. Under orders, Gamygyn can make these spirits appear and speak with his controller. He also teaches the sciences.

Glasyalabolas appears as a dog with wings. When properly controlled and subdued he can convey knowledge of all the arts and sciences instantaneously. He is a particularly unpleasant and dangerous demon who incites people to commit murder and to injure one another. He can convey the gift of invisibility when ordered, provided that he is fully and firmly controlled.

Gomory appears as a very beautiful woman when summoned. She wears a sparkling, bejewelled crown. Her main powers are to procure attractive female partners, but she can also locate hidden treasures and answer questions about future possibilities.

Guison is cynocephalic, meaning dog-headed. This demon can answer questions about the past and present, as well as offer a range of future possibilities. He can bestow honours and social ranks and reconcile enemies should his controller order him to do so.

Glasyalabolas, a particularly dangerous demon who incites people to commit murder and to injure one another.

Hagenti appears as a gigantic winged bull when summoned, but will assume human form when ordered. He has the power to bestow wisdom and can transmute base metals into gold. He also has the odd ability to turn wine into water.

Halpas appears as a dove when summoned, but is far from peaceful. He arranges for the wicked to be killed in battle, and burns down towns and cities. When ordered to do so by his controlling witch or wizard, Halpas is able to create fortresses and fill them with soldiers.

Ipos appears as an angel with the head of a lion. He has a small tail like a rabbit or hare. He also has webbed feet resembling those of a water bird. His gifts, when he is under proper control, are quick-wittedness and courage. He will also answer questions and present a range of future possibilities.

Larajie looks like a demonic version of Robin Hood. He wears a green tunic and carries a bow and a quiver of arrows. He causes wars and battles, and makes arrow wounds putrefy.

Malpas arrives in the form of a large crow, but assumes human form when commanded to do so. Being able to arrive in crow-like form, his voice is harsh, almost a croaking sound. When skilled work needs to be done urgently, Malpas can bring craftsmen of all kinds from any part of the world to help. When told to do so by his controller, Malpas can destroy the thoughts of his enemies.

Marbas can appear either as a lion or in human form. He has the power both to cause illness and to cure it, and will do whatever his controller asks in that direction. As well as his power over disease, he is a skilled engineer and mechanic and can give information on how such tasks can best be performed. He can change human beings into other forms if ordered to do so by his controller.

Marchosias appears as a winged wolf, breathing fire, and has a long serpentine tail. Like most of the other demons, he can assume human form when his controller orders him to. He is very powerful and formidable in

Marbas in the form of a lion. He has the power both to cause illness and to cure it.

battle and, surprising for a demon, he will remain loyal and faithful to the magician who has summoned him.

Morax resembles a bull with a human head. Once under control, he will help by teaching science and the secrets of the stars. He is also very knowledgeable about herbs and gems.

Murmur appears as a soldier mounted on a flying griffin. Once under control he will teach philosophy, and he can command the spirits of the departed to appear. He is also able to make the spirits answer questions posed by his controlling witch or wizard.

Naberius appears in the form of a cockerel and tends to flutter around the magic circle when summoned. Under the control of his summoner, he can give skills in arts and sciences to the coven, and teach rhetoric. He also has the power to restore lost titles, honours, and social ranks when his controller directs him.

Orias appears as a lion riding a great charger. He holds two great snakes in his huge and powerful right paw, and he himself has the tail of a serpent. Under the control of the witch or wizard who has summoned him, Orias can bestow ranks and titles and teach people about the stars.

Orobas makes his entry as a spirited horse, but changes to human form when commanded. He can answer questions about the past and the present and offer guidance concerning future possibilities. He is an expert on the details of the creation of the universe, and will answer questions about it. Again, unlike most demons, he is totally loyal to the witch or wizard who has summoned him and will protect his summoner from temptation from other demons.

Ose is a demon who favours appearing as a leopard just as Flauros does, but he soon assumes human form. He can endow people with scientific skill and change people into any form or shape that his controller asks for – without the people knowing that they have been changed!

Paimon, a demon king of great power, is particularly loyal to Lucifer. He appears wearing his crown, heralded by musicians. He rides on a camel and his voice roars like thunder. He is one of the greatest of the demonic teachers and can impart amazing knowledge of both arts and sciences. It is not always easy for the magician who summons him to understand him because of his loud, roaring voice.

Phoenix appears looking like the mythological bird of the same name. He sings in a soft, sweet voice — very different from the voice of Paimon. At the magician's order, Phoenix will assume human form. He teaches science and has great knowledge of it. He is also an outstandingly good poet. He obeys the magician amiably and willingly and, for a demon, is almost pleasant!

Procel appears in the guise of an angel. He is another skilled teacher of science and geometry. He is capable of making vast disturbances accompanied by the noise of rushing water. Because of his command over water, he is often called upon by his summoner to temper bath water and keep it gently warm.

Purson is a demon in the form of a lion-headed man, who rides a fierce bear just as Balam does. Purson can conceal and uncover treasures, and can answer questions about the past, the present, and future possibilities when ordered to do so by his summoner.

Raum arrives in the form of a gigantic rook, or crow, when summoned, just as Malpas does. He then assumes human shape. He can locate and steal treasure for the witch or wizard who has summoned him. Raum is a very destructive demon who can be launched by his summoner against any city. He can procure attractive and willing sex partners for his summoner, or for one of his summoner's companions, if asked.

Ronobe appears in the form of an awesome monster that usually instills fright into anyone who sees it. Despite his traumatizing appearance, however, he is one of the more biddable demons and willingly teaches rhetoric and the arts to the group of magicians working with the summoner. He also teaches them languages.

Sabanack appears as a fully armed and equipped soldier on horseback. He has a lion's head above a human body. His major function consists of building fortifications of all kinds. His main horror — extended toward his summoner's enemies — is to inflict them with putrefying sores filled with worms and maggots, which eventually prove both agonizing and fatal.

Saleos arrives in the form of a soldier riding a crocodile in the same way that Agares does. His main function is to find attractive and willing sex partners for the summoner and his colleagues in the coven.

Seere arrives on a magnificently powerful winged horse — very much like Pegasus — when he is summoned. Seere himself is equally attractive. He is amoral, rather than immoral, seemingly indifferent to both good and evil. His main function when the summoner commands him is speed: he can transport his witch, or wizard, or a selected coven member, to any distant spot almost immediately. He is also the best of all paranormal policemen and detectives: he detects thieves instantaneously.

Separ appears as a fully armed and equipped soldier dressed all in red in much the same way that Berith does. He influences women sexually, so that they will go in pursuit of male partners.

Shax appears in the form of a dove when summoned, but unlike the other dove-demon, Halpas, is far from peaceful or pleasant. He is all too ready and eager to destroy the mind, sight, and hearing of any person against whom the witch or wizard launches him. Shax will steal when told to do so, and will transport people or things when his summoner orders it.

Sytry does not appear as a complete leopard like Flauros and Ose. Sytry has the head of a leopard on a human body. He is another sex-demon, who urges nubile young women to appear naked, and then finds male partners for them.

Valac is a complete contrast. He appears as an angelic little boy and flies in on a two-headed dragon when summoned by a witch or wizard. When asked about buried treasures, he gives truthful and honest answers about their location and also helps his summoner to capture serpents when they are required for the coven's spells. Valac locates the snakes, renders them docile, and then fetches them to his controller.

Valefor comes to his summoner in the guise of a multi-headed lion. His main work of temptation is to lead human beings to commit theft and then abandon them to their arrest and punishment.

Vapula has the appearance of a winged lion. When summoned and fully under control, he teaches people many important manual skills, such as weaving, embroidery, carpentry, and stonemasonry. He also teaches science and philosophy.

Vassago is scarcely a demon at all in the sense that demons are either downright evil and malevolent or, at their best, mischievous and a serious nuisance. He seems to be genuinely good-natured, and white magicians also call upon his aid. His main talent is helping people to recover what they have lost. He is often referred to by magicians as the "prince of prophecy."

Vepar appears as a mermaid when summoned. He is very much a sea demon, and causes storms that take ships and sailors to the depths of the ocean. In addition to drowning his summoner's enemies, he also kills by infecting them with putrefying sores full of worms and maggots.

Vine is another of the demons who prefer to appear in horrifying monstrous forms and then change into human shapes when commanded to do so by the magician who has summoned them. Vine's talents include finding things that are hidden, revealing the real identity of witches, wizards, Satanists, and black magicians, and building fortifications when ordered to by his summoner. He is also capable of creating storms at sea.

Vual arrives as a camel – not simply riding one! He speaks in ancient Egyptian when questioned, and procures attractive women as sex partners for coven members. He is also capable of acting as an oracle and giving advice to his summoner.

Zagan, when fully under control, is a particularly useful demon. He appears as a flying bull, and his gifts to his summoner and the coven members include quick-wittedness. His greatest talent is thought to be his ability to make fools wise when ordered to by his controller. He can change any old metal into coin of the realm for them, and can also change water into wine or oil.

These then are the celebrated seventy-two demons who were imprisoned at one time by the power of Solomon's seal according to the legend.

14
Satanism in Salem

If the closing decade of the seventeenth century can be regarded as part of relatively modern history, then the infamous Salem witch trials are uncomfortably close to our own time. Referred to briefly in Chapter 9 in connection with the use of the name Beelzebub, the Salem phenomena demand a more extensive treatment in any comprehensive study of Satanism.

The Salem witch trials were a series of hearings held before local magistrates that led to county court trials in the days when Massachusetts was a colony. The trials covered the prosecution of innocent victims accused of witchcraft in the counties of Essex, Suffolk, and Middlesex, in Massachusetts, from February 1692 until May of the following year.

Although popularly associated with the name "Salem," the trials extended through Ipswich and Andover as well as Salem Town. In 1692 they were held in the Court of Oyer and Terminer. This is a legal term that requires further explanation. The phrase originated in English law and meant a commission by which an assize judge sat to prosecute criminal offences of a serious type. The words came originally from French law, where it was called *audiendo et terminando*, meaning "to hear and determine," or "decide."

Close to 160 people were arrested and imprisoned in 1692, and several more were accused. Half a dozen of these innocent victims died in prison.

In 1693, the Superior Court of Judicature met in Salem, Boston, Charlestown, and Ipswich. Only three convictions resulted from thirty-one witchcraft trials conducted in the Superior Court. Between them, however, the courts convicted twenty-nine innocent victims at a time when witchcraft was regarded as a capital felony. Nineteen innocent people were hanged: fourteen women and five men. One hero, Giles Corey, refused to plead and was crushed to death to try to force him to plead.

Some innocent victims died in prison.

Mass hysteria of the kind that contributed to the Salem witch trials tends to break out when people are sensitive to serious dangers in their environment and when there are grim political uncertainties. The Royal Charter of Massachusetts was cancelled when James II ascended the English throne. In 1684, James installed Sir Edmund Andros as governor of what he styled the Dominion of New England. Andros was thrown out in 1689 when James II was dethroned in what was always referred to by English historians as "The Glorious Revolution." Then William and Mary came to the throne.

Tension was growing between the English colonists and groups of indigenous Americans along the Atlantic seaboard. There were problems in getting various new Massachusetts charters settled and approved, and this led to a vacuum in some of the legal systems. There was significant legal argument, for example, in 1690, when a group of pirates were tried, condemned, and executed on the authority of what was then called the Court of Assistants. In 1692, new courts, justices of the peace, and sheriffs were appointed in a hurry. At this time the new court of Oyer and Terminer that was central to the Salem witch trials was established.

Other factors contributed to the social pressures and uncertainties in the Salem area. Salem Village was distinct from Salem Town, and the residents of Salem Village wanted their own church, separate from and independent of the Salem Town church. They finally got their wish in 1689, but it only increased the social tensions and pressures. Opinions were angrily divided about whether or not Salem Village wanted Samuel Parris as their minister, and about whether or not to give him the deed of the minister's residence as part of his clerical remuneration.

Despite all their problems fighting with indigenous Americans, and the difficulties of producing satisfactory farm crops, the colonists' family sizes were increasing. This led to continual disputes about land ownership. As families grew, generation by generation, there was insufficient land to support them. Farmers began pushing inland, which created more wars with the indigenous inhabitants.

The puritanical religious fanaticism of many of the colonists made matters far worse. If crops failed, livestock died, or earthquakes and foul weather hit them, they tended to think that someone's sin had made God angry. Part of their witch-hunting was aimed at finding and punishing the "evildoers" who were annoying God.

At this time, the puritans were all too vehemently active as a group inside the Anglican Church: they did not like using the Book of Common Prayer; they disapproved of priestly robes; and they did not want to kneel during the Eucharist. These puritan fanatics were a political group as well as a religious one, and their reasons for emigrating as colonists were often political as well as religious. At the time of the Salem witch trials, Massachusetts was very much a religio-political puritan colony.

The Reverend Cotton Mather was a prominent influence at the time of the Salem trials. A dangerous misogynist and a fanatical believer in witchcraft and black magic, Mather bore a significant share of guilt for the deaths of the innocent victims of the trials. In 1689 he had written a book entitled *Memorable Providences Relating to Witchcrafts and Possessions* in the course of which he described how, in his opinion, four children of a Boston stonemason were bewitched by an Irish washerwoman named Mary Glover.

Another contributory factor to the Salem tragedy was the puritanical *social* climate prevailing in seventeenth-century Massachusetts. It was very much a patriarchal society. Women were seen as subservient to men, and were suspected of being in league with the devil because they were "lustful by nature" — misogynistic nonsense paralleled in Kramer's *Malleus Maleficarum*, a text which would have been avidly studied by puritans who believed in witchcraft.

Another grim perspective of the social context in Salem at the time was the property law, which stated that if no legal heir could be found, the land reverted to its previous owner, or in his absence, to the colony. Witch-hunting was almost invariably directed against unmarried women and widows who owned land. If they could be successfully prosecuted and executed, their accusers — if they were the previous landowners — stood to regain the land. Apparently, killing "witches" could bring great wealth!

The events leading up to the witch trials seem to have begun with two young girls: Abigail Williams, aged eleven, and Betty Parris, aged nine. They were the niece and daughter of the Reverend Samuel Parris, who had numerous enemies in Salem. The two girls had fits resembling severe epilepsy. They crawled under furniture, made weird noises, twisted their bodies into very odd shapes, threw objects about, and said that they were being nipped as if with invisible pincers and jabbed with unseen sharp objects.

The Reverend Deodat Lawson had been a minister in Salem Village from 1684 to 1688. He reported that members of his family had died there because of Satanism and witchcraft, and he produced an eyewitness account of the strange behaviour of Abigail and Betty. When he preached in Salem, he was interrupted by the actions of some of the enchanted girls — which probably included Mary Walcott, who was destined to feature later in the episode of the witch-cake. Dr. William Griggs examined them and then gave his opinion that there were no *medical* causes of their odd behaviour: in his opinion, it had to be witchcraft.

Sarah Good, Sarah Osborne, and a female slave named Tituba were all accused of witchcraft, and of causing the odd behaviour of the supposedly enchanted girls. Sarah Osborne had a reputation for sexual behaviour that contravened the hypocritical puritanical standards of Salem. Sarah Good was a homeless beggar, and the hapless Tituba was at a massive disadvantage as far as the residents of Salem were concerned because of her ethnic difference. All of them were very vulnerable to accusations of witchcraft, and there was no one who was prepared to defend them. The local magistrates interrogated them for several days, starting on March 1, 1692. They were then imprisoned.

Martha Corey, Rebecca Nurse, young Dorothy Good, and Rachel Clinton were arrested later. Martha was a very sensible and practical woman, who had said that she did not believe what the supposedly enchanted girls were saying about witchcraft. It was her misfortune that her common sense and honesty drew unfavourable attention in a community that was convinced that witchcraft existed.

There were serious doubts and conflicts of opinion in the locality because both Martha and Rebecca were respectable church members. It was argued that if such upright and God-fearing citizens could be witches, then who was above suspicion? Dorothy Good was only four years old, yet her supposed testimony was regarded as a confession – one that implicated her mother, as well! Rachel was arrested in Ipswich at the end of March, but the charges against her were not linked to the Salem girls.

Things got worse in April when Sarah Cloyce (the sister of Rebecca Nurse) and Elizabeth Proctor were arrested and brought before two magistrates, Hathorne and Corwin, who were also high-ranking members of the Governor's Council. Deputy Governor Thomas Danforth was also at the interrogation. For the first time since the proceedings had begun, John Proctor stood up and objected. He was then arrested!

Martha's husband, Giles, Abigail Hobbs, Bridget Bishop, and Mary Warren were also arrested. Mary was a servant of the Proctors. Deliverance Hobbs, Abigail's stepmother, was also arrested. She, Mary, and Deliverance all pleaded guilty *and began naming their accomplices!* The people whom they named were duly arrested and charged. Nehemiah Abbott was one of them, but was released when the accusers said that he had not been among those who had bewitched them. Mary Eastey was not so lucky. At first the accusers said that she was not one of those responsible: then they got together and changed their minds. Mary was re-arrested!

More and more accusations of witchcraft flooded in, but word had spread about the danger of these mindless charges, and many of those accused wisely took to their heels. Two of these prudent escapees were George Jacobs and Daniel Andrews: neither was apprehended.

The situation worsened dramatically on May 27, 1692, when the Special Court of Oyer and Terminer was set up for the counties of Essex, Suffolk, and Middlesex. More and more warrants were issued, but Sarah Osborne had the relative good luck to die in jail on May 10, 1692, before anything worse could happen to her at the hands of the puritan fanatics.

The Salem witchcraft hysteria continued to worsen. By May 31, 1692, there were more than sixty people in custody charged with witchcraft.

The unpleasant and interfering Reverend Cotton Mather wrote to Judge John Richards on May 31, 1692, expressing his wholehearted and enthusiastic support for the witchcraft prosecutions. He also told the judge that it was dangerous to rely solely on what was referred to as "spectral evidence," and gave him large amounts of advice on ways in which the court could successfully pursue the cases against the accused.

The Court of Oyer and Terminer opened in Salem Town on June 2, 1692. The chief magistrate was the new lieutenant governor, William Stoughton. The prosecuting attorney was Thomas Newton. The Clerk to the Court was Stephen Sewall.

The hapless Bridget Bishop was tried first, found guilty, and duly hanged on June 10. Sarah Good, Elizabeth Howe, Susannah Martin, Sarah Wildes, and Rebecca Nurse were all tried, found guilty, and executed on July 19.

George Burroughs was about to be executed when he tried to prove his innocence by reciting the Lord's Prayer. It was firmly believed by witch-persecuting fanatics that no witch or wizard who had sold his soul to the devil would be able to do this. Some of the crowd were very impressed and were on the verge of interfering with the execution on Burroughs's behalf when the ubiquitous Cotton Mather stuck his nose in again. He settled the crowd by explaining that Burroughs had to be guilty because he had been declared so by a jury — and the jury could not be wrong! Along with Martha Carrier, George Jacobs, John Willard, and John Proctor, George Burroughs was duly hanged.

Eight more innocent victims were hanged on September 22, 1692, and Giles Corey, who had stubbornly refused to plead, was pressed to death. This was a technique that was used to force a prisoner to say whether he was guilty or innocent. It was technically referred to as the *peine forte et dure* and consisted of adding increasingly heavy stones to the victim's chest. Corey, a tough and determined old hero, stubbornly refused to plead. Nicholas Noyes, a puritanical minister of much the same stamp as Cotton Mather, referred to the eight innocent victims of this latest bout of witchcraft hysteria as "eight firebrands of Hell."

Governor Phipps then contacted Cotton Mather in September and commissioned him to write up an account of the trials in depth and detail, which he did with alacrity — and the help of court clerk Stephen Sewall, who was a close friend and supplied him with all the official documents needed. Mather's book on the Salem trials was called *Wonders of the Invisible World*.

Governor Phipps stood the court down in October 1692, but things continued in 1693, although something approaching sanity and common sense was now beginning to be discernible. In January 1693, the Superior Court of Judicature met in Salem. It was headed by William Stoughton, with Anthony Checkley as attorney general. Jonathan Elatson was appointed to be clerk of court.

The first five cases that came before the court were those of Sarah Buckley, Margaret and Rebecca Jacobs, Mary Whittredge, and Job Tookey. All were exonerated. Many of those who were still in jail were cleared by grand juries. Three, however, were found guilty. These were Elizabeth Johnson, Sarah Wardwell, and Mary Post. Stoughton duly wrote out warrants for their executions — Governor Phipps promptly pardoned them and saved their lives.

Five more innocent victims of the now-fading witchcraft hysteria were tried at the end of January and beginning of February. These five were: Sarah Cole, Lydia and Sarah Dustin, Mary Taylor, and Mary Toothaker. All were found not guilty, but were forced to remain in prison until their jail fees had been paid. Lydia died there on March 10, 1693.

Things were definitely seen to be improving when Captain John Alden was cleared at the end of April when the court convened in Suffolk County. Even better news came when Mary Watkins, a servant girl, was charged for bringing false charges of witchcraft against her employer. The witchcraft hysteria was now almost over, but it had had tragic consequences for many innocent people.

What exactly were the so-called legal procedures that were employed during the Salem witch trials?

If a person thought that some negative event such as crop failure, disease, a serious accident, or death was the result of witchcraft, then he or she would tell the local magistrates, and name the suspect. If the magistrates thought that the complaint was reasonable — and under the influence of puritanical bigots like Cotton Mather, they often did — the accused witch would be arrested. Then came an interrogation and a public examination, including a search of the accused's body for traditional "witch marks." The accused would be urged to confess.

In cases where local magistrates believed that there *was* a case to answer — and this happened far too often — the accused was passed to a higher court. Once that happened, a grand jury would be assembled and witnesses would be called to testify. The charges were afflicting a victim with witchcraft, or making a covenant with Satan.

Even after death, the accused were given neither sympathy nor respect. After being hanged, their bodies were cut down and more or less thrown into shallow graves well away from consecrated ground. After the crowd filtered away, their families would exhume their loved ones after dark and rebury them reverently and secretly on private family land.

One of the great problems in the Salem witch trials was so-called spectral evidence, wherein the person complaining of being bewitched said that he or she could see a spectral outline of the accused whenever any of the ill effects of witchcraft were felt. It was argued before the court by various self-styled experts on witchcraft and Satanism that a witch or wizard had to give Satan permission to use their shadowy spectral representation before such a spectral form could be revealed to the person being bewitched.

Those who were opposed to convicting the accused on the basis of such spectral evidence were of the opinion that Satan had the power to use the shape of anyone he chose, irrespective of whether that person had given permission for it to be used. It was also suggested that Satan might well use the spectral form of some staunch and devout Christian in order to get that person accused of witchcraft and black magic. It was at this point in the debate that Cotton Mather, his equally obsessed father, Increase Mather, and a few like-minded puritan fanatics urged the court to find additional evidence in case the spectral evidence was too weak to secure a conviction. Spectral evidence was later ruled inadmissible, and this may have helped to bring the witch hysteria to an end in the Salem area.

A confession from the accused was considered acceptable evidence that the person was a witch or wizard (and indulging in Satanism). If the accused's premises were searched, and poppets (witch dolls) were found (or surreptitiously planted there by enemies of the accused), that was also taken as evidence against them. If the searchers located any books, such as grimoires, or texts on palmistry and astrology, those books were regarded as evidence that witchcraft was taking place in the accused's home.

Just as damning as the discovery of suspect books was the discovery of a jar of ointment. This was almost certain to be some totally innocuous, home-made salve to relieve rheumatism or arthritis or to get rid of a rash, but it could get an innocent girl hanged as a witch. The search of the accused's body for witch marks — any mole or birthmark was enough to get an innocent person executed — was another acceptable form of evidence. A variation of this was the discovery by the accusers that there was an insensitive place on the accused's body. After the indignity and discomfort of being stripped and continuously searched and prodded for hours by the accusers, it was highly likely that the accused would fail to register sensation at some points on the skin. Such failure to experience sensation was acceptable evidence of witchcraft.

One of the strangest attempts to track down the supposed witches during the Salem hysteria consisted of making a witch cake. In February 1692, Mary Sibly, who was the aunt of Mary Walcott (another of the girls who behaved oddly and claimed that it was because she was afflicted by witchcraft) ordered one of her slaves to make a witch cake. The slave concerned was John Indian, who was believed to have special knowledge of white magic and could, therefore, help to trace the witch who was responsible for Mary Walcott's weird, enchanted behaviour.

John duly made a witch cake in the traditional way — from rye mixed with some urine from the supposedly afflicted girls. The witch cake was then fed to a dog.

The theory behind the witch cake white magic was that when a dog bit the cake, the witch would scream in pain! The strange folklore hypothesis behind this witch cake detection method was that when a witch or wizard sent out a magic spell to harm someone, microscopically small particles of that witch worked their way into the person being bewitched. This theory ties in with ideas about the way that witches and wizards use the so-called "evil eye," because it was also believed that these invisibly tiny, toxic, malignant particles came from the witch's *eyes* when she looked at the person who was being bewitched.

The next part of the hypothesis was that some of those minute evil particles of the witch who had afflicted the girls would leave the victim's body in her urine. Once this "infected" urine was mixed with rye and fed to a dog, the witch would feel pain while the dog chewed particles of her that were in the cake! As the witch screamed with pain, she would immediately be detected as the evil person who had afflicted the girls.

When the Reverend Parris, uncle to Abigail Williams and father of Betty Parris, who both claimed to have been bewitched, found out what Mary Sibly had done, he denounced *all* types of magic — even white magic of the type that John Indian had performed on Mary's orders!

The Reverend Parris explained to Mary — and his Salem congregation — that trying to use magic against magic was foolish and wrong because all magic (in his opinion) came from the devil. So using magic of one type against another was like trying to use the devil to attack the devil. When Parris used this argument, he was probably thinking of what Jesus had said when he had been spitefully accused by the scribes and Pharisees of casting out devils by using Beelzebub, the prince of devils (Matthew 12:22-29).

A very similar argument was used during the trial of Elizabeth Howe, one of the five innocent victims hanged on July 19, 1692. Elizabeth had been accused of killing some animals by using witchcraft against them. It was suggested that an ear be cut from each animal's carcass and burned. If minute evil particles of Elizabeth were in the animals' ears, she would scream in pain as those "infected" ears were burned.

It was said in some accounts that the female slave, Tituba, was accused of teaching the girls voodoo in the Parris kitchen, but there is little or no first-hand evidence of this. Several secondary sources suggest that she did, and that some of the girls used egg white and a mirror to try to find out what their future husbands would do for a living. A coffin was said to have formed in the egg white during one of these supposed fortune-telling occasions, which understandably frightened the girls!

When tried with Sarah Good and Sarah Osborne, however, Tituba is recorded as having spoken about "invisible creatures" and strange rituals "binding them in the service of Satan." She also said that a number of other people were engaged in "the devil's conspiracy." Testimony of that kind in the ethos of the Salem witch trials was a short cut to a rope and the nearest convenient tree.

More supposed evidence against the accused consisted of a touch test. Basically, it was believed that the tiny evil particles that afflicted the witch's victims radiated out from the witch's eyes. If the witch was blindfolded, no particles could escape and infect the victim. Some of the accused were therefore blindfolded and led to the allegedly afflicted girls, who were screaming and writhing about dramatically to show that they were bewitched. The particle theory argued that the tiny evil specks had come originally from the witch and had entered the victim to make her behave weirdly. As the particles were part of the witch, it was believed that they would be drawn back into her if she touched a bewitched victim. According to some of the records, when a blindfolded accused touched the afflicted girls, they conveniently stopped screaming and writhing and declared that they now felt well again!

There were several interesting aftermaths, once the Salem witchcraft hysteria had burnt itself out. On August 25, 1706, Ann Putnam, who had been a strident accuser, asked humbly for forgiveness. She said that she had never acted out of malice toward any of the accused, who she now knew were innocent. She claimed that she had been deluded by Satan into thinking that these harmless and innocent people — whom she had helped to destroy — were witches and wizards. In 1712, the Reverend Nicholas Noyes and his church members in Salem cancelled their excommunications of the late Rebecca Nurse and heroic Giles Corey, both victims of the witchcraft hysteria.

The Salem witchcraft phenomena raise a number of significant questions as to their *real* cause. Psychologically, it has been suggested that the constant battles against indigenous Americans had brought on some form of anxiety neurosis or hysteria among the Massachusetts settlers.

The suspicion of ergot poisoning is one that cannot be easily dismissed. Ergot poisoning, or ergotism, is the result of ingesting the alkaloids produced by a fungus known as *Claviceps purpurea*, which infects rye and some other cereals. *Lysergic acid diethylamide*, or LSD, has many powerful effects, including hallucinations and time distortions. It was first synthesized in 1938 from ergot fungus by Albert Hofmann. Ergotism can also produce convulsions.

If the apparently afflicted girls in Salem had been exposed to ergotine, it would easily explain most of their so-called "witchcraft" symptoms. The strongest argument against this theory is that ergotine poisoning tends to infect everyone in a household — and the girls experiencing the strange symptoms of "enchantment" were not in the same household, nor were other members of their households similarly affected.

The deep sleep experiences of which some afflicted girls complained might have been caused by *encephalitis lethargica*, which can be carried by birds.

What if it was something nastier, but far simpler: spite, jealousy, resentment, dislike of someone and a desire to get even?

The final possibility is the most sinister: if witchcraft and black magic really exist, and if they can really work to the detriment of human victims, was something truly evil and uncanny happening in Salem at the end of the seventeenth century?

Not that the accused of that hopelessly twisted legal processes were anything other than totally innocent victims — but what if *something* or *someone* had real magical power and malicious intent? Could anything be more evil than the damnable processes that led some people to feel that they were genuinely bewitched — and to go on to accuse the innocent in a way that led to their deaths? Was Ann Putnam right when she thought that the devil had deluded her into thinking that some of her totally innocent neighbours were witches?

Demon Reports: A Survey

Nearly one thousand reports of alleged cases of demon-associated phenomena were analyzed by the authors in March 2010. During the process, the phenomena were divided into ten separate categories, and were later analyzed according to the areas of Britain from whence the reports came.

The first category dealt with incubus (male demon) and succubus (female demon) reports. These were very few and far between, but it seemed likely that more cases existed than were actually reported because witnesses were embarrassed by such encounters.

The second category covered reports of black magic, witchcraft, wizardry, sorcery, necromancy, Satanism, cursed people, cursed objects, and cursed locations involving Satan, Lucifer, Beelzebub, or other demons and evil spirits.

The third group of reports included people who believed that they had been possessed by demons or other evil entities. These reports again were few and far between, and it seemed probable to the researchers that many more potential reports were not forthcoming because of the near impossibility of distinguishing between mental illness and supposed demon possession.

Category four dealt with ancient legends involving bizarre structural traumas: buildings being moved; bridges being miraculously constructed or destroyed in a very short time; deep holes appearing without apparent natural geological cause; monoliths or henges being raised, moved, or flattened suddenly by demonic powers. These events are almost invariably ascribed to the devil himself. They serve as "explanations" for curious phenomena that people living at the time were unable to explain rationally and scientifically. They are included in the analysis because there are still lingering beliefs that the miraculous, demonic cause of the event just *might* be true! These legends are very widespread, and more than one hundred cases were recorded.

Category five deals with hell hounds, which are widely and frequently reported. Close to two hundred cases were brought to the researchers' attention, from all over Britain, of witnesses seeing these demons, or dangerous evil entities, that appear in the form of huge black dogs with glowing red eyes.

The sixth category refers to demons or evil entities associated with water. These, too, are surprisingly common, and close to one hundred cases have been reported throughout Britain. Kelpies and other types of water demons either attempt to lure their potential victims into dangerous waters to attack them, or push them from a bank or cliff top into the water.

The seventh group of demonic reports covers repulsive entities, variously referred to as ghouls, boggarts, werebeasts, shapeshifters, and afrits. Some entities in this category, such as the banshee, are heard rather than seen.

Category eight includes actual encounters with Satan, Lucifer, Mephistopheles, Beelzebub, and other devils, plus familiars, imps, minor demons, and other evil entities.

The ninth category covers miscellaneous experiences that were reported to the investigators: patches of mist which conveyed an evil atmosphere; malevolent tingling sensations like electric shocks; or feelings of being touched by something invisible and unfriendly.

Category ten includes reports of monsters described in the legends as "worms" and "dragons" that had dangerous, hostile intentions toward human beings, and seemed to be demonic in origin.

As well as arranging this demonic research into categories, we concentrated on the geographical locations from which examples came. Argyle and Bute had a number of interesting cases. MacKinnon's Cave on the Isle of Mull is named after an unfortunate piper who explored the cave and was pursued by an ogress, or demoness, who lived there. She is said to have killed MacKinnon when his music failed to please her.

Another very aggressive and unpleasant demonic monster, an extremely ugly brute, was reported from Grador Rock near Balvaig. A local fisherman ventured too close to the monstrosity, which promptly killed him.

Two fishermen reportedly had a miraculous escape when the demonic monster of Gare Loch suddenly reared itself nine metres out of the water and swam rapidly toward them. They rowed desperately to the shore, leaped out of their boat, and ran inland. The monster did not pursue them, but swam back to the centre of the loch and dived out of sight.

A party of huntsmen on the shores of Gare Loch were attacked by a fierce demonic monster that killed three of them with its heavy tail and knocked down a number of trees around the shores of the loch. The surviving huntsmen ran inland and climbed large trees that would be proof against the monster's tail swings.

Near the Burn of Inbhirinneoin, in Glen Lyon, is an ancient burial mound that legend says is one of the gateways to hell. A strange being, part-human, part-demon has been reported occasionally from the area as if he is the gatekeeper.

A very strange legend is associated with the monastery on the Isle of Iona, which has an otherwise unsurpassed reputation for sanctity and holiness. According to the legend, when the monastery was being built, the construction work was persistently interrupted by the devil. Saint Columba was consulted and had a vision that informed him that the only way to prevent Satan from interfering with the work was to build the monastery over the body of a human sacrifice.

This legend sounds remarkably like a curious hybrid of early Christianity and old pagan ideas. A very good and holy follower of Columba by the name of Odran volunteered to help, and was duly buried alive in the place where the monastery was to be built. Three days after his burial, Columba exhumed him – only to see that Odran was still alive! There are two versions of the legend. In the first, his overjoyed companions welcome him back into their fellowship, where he eventually achieves high rank in the church. In the second, darker, version, Odran declares: "There is no surprise in death – and hell need not be feared!" Columba promptly reburies him, ensuring that his mouth is filled with soil. The monastery is then constructed without further interference from Satan.

Another unpleasant demon is reportedly to be found in the area near Moy Castle, on the Isle of Mull. The creature, known as the Beannighe, is seen washing clothes – but this is an ill omen, as the clothes belong to someone who is doomed to die. On one occasion in the Middle Ages, the castle owner saw the Beannighe washing his clothes: he died in battle next day!

In the Lochgilphead area, a resident woke in the night to find herself being strangled by an invisible demon. With great courage and presence of mind she fought back and the evil spirit – possibly an incubus – vanished. The next day a priest was called in to exorcise the house.

By the Cladach-a-Chrogain beach in the Tiree area, there are frequent reports of a hideous demonic hell hound. The local name for such evil entities is Cusith. Like spirits at Victorian seances, the Cusith conveys his meaning numerically. If he barks once or twice, all is well. However, if he emits *three* blood-curdling barks, death and disaster are coming. Part of his legend is that he can become part human in form on occasion, and when this happens his warnings are more terrible than when he delivers them in his hound shape.

The ruined kirk (church) in Alloway, in Ayrshire, has a very sinister reputation. A strange, dark, demonic mist drifts toward it periodically, accompanied by a sinister sound like a barrel rolling over stones. The ruined church has been the site of a suicide, and the body of a homeless man was found in the vicinity – cause of death unknown. There is also an account of a child having been murdered in the locality.

Knockdolian Castle in the Colmonell area has reportedly been cursed by a sinister water demon. Originally in the innocuous form of an attractive mermaid, this water demon would sit on a black rock in the water near the castle. For some inexplicable reason, the castle owner ordered the rock to be destroyed so that the mermaid could no longer sit on it. Driven to fury by the destruction of her rock, the mermaid cursed the family, declaring that no heir of theirs would inherit Knockdolian Castle. Historically, it is interesting to note that it passed into the hands of the McCubbins. Equally interesting is the derivation of the name of their lands, which were known at one time as Trudonag from the early Welsh Gaelic. The name *Trudonag* translates as "Home of the Betony" – the betony herb was widely used as protection against demons, evil-spirits, and witches!

A very formidable demon was reported from the area of Dundonald Castle in Ayrshire. The witness described it as being humanoid in shape, more than three metres tall, covered in thick, dark hair, and having glaring red eyes. Very wisely she watched it from a safe distance, and made no attempt to get any closer.

Torrylin Cairn is a very ancient chambered tomb near Kilmory, on the Isle of Arran. According to local myths and legends, together with reports from witnesses, strange, shadowy, spectral, demonic entities stand guard over the tomb and put fiendish curses on anyone who attempts to remove anything from the cairn.

A demonic evil spirit that was once a witch who was tortured to obtain her confession and then burned at the stake in the vicinity of Mag Lane in Hockliffe in Bedfordshire has been reported by numerous witnesses. Her misty outline drifts along the lane as if looking for nervous witnesses to frighten.

In 1340, when the Church of St. Mary the Virgin at Marston Moretaine in Bedfordshire was being built, legend says that Satan attempted to steal the bell tower, but found that it was too heavy even for his massive strength, and had to set it down again. Tower and church remain separate to this day.

Odell in Bedfordshire dates back to Saxon times, when it was part of the property of Levenot, one of King Edward the Confessor's Thanes. Its original title was Wadehelle, or Wadelle, and it meant "the hill where woad grows." Woad was an interesting dye-making plant that the early Britons used to stain their bodies. Julius Caesar commented on it. The woad plant is known as *Isatis tinctoria* and the blue dye extracted from it makes what is referred to as "magician's ink" when it is dissolved in pure alcohol. This so-called magician's ink is used by some witches and wizards to write out spells and incantations. In legend, Sir Roland Alston of Odell made a pact with Satan. When the time came for the devil to collect Roland's soul, he ran to All Saints Church to try to obtain help and avoid this part of the bargain. The devil got the better of him, and Roland was duly dragged off to hell. For several centuries afterward, there were five drag marks in the stone porch of All Saints, allegedly made by Satan pulling at the reluctant Roland. More recently, they have been cemented over during church renovation work.

St. Mary's Church in Aldworth in Berkshire has a similar story to tell. John Everafraid, as he was nicknamed, made a pact with Satan, and then avoided paying his dues. His contract with the devil stated that Lucifer could have his soul whether he was buried inside or outside the church. He cunningly left instructions that he was to be buried *under the wall* of St. Mary's, so that when Beelzebub came to claim him, he was neither *inside* nor *outside* the church — thus invalidating the diabolical contract.

The devil is often referred to as Grim in legends and place names, and this seems to be the case at Grim's Ditch near Ashampstead Green in Berkshire. Well over eight kilometres long, this ancient cutting may have been used to demarcate a property boundary, or to have been part of a defensive earthwork. However, Grim was also used to refer to Woden or Odin, as well as to Satan. Woden was a war-god among his many roles, and his name could also be translated as "the god in the mask." Naming the ditch after him, rather than after Satan or Lucifer argues in favour of its once having had a military purpose.

Hoe Benham is close to Newbury in Berkshire and is reputedly troubled by what witnesses once described as the ghost of a large spectral pig. A ghostly sheep has also been seen there. These are regarded in some accounts as demonic entities and perhaps in the case of the phantom pig there are links with the Gadarene Swine as recorded in the New Testament (Luke 8:6-39). Jesus healed the possessed man, and the evil spirits that had possessed him went into the swine. They then stampeded downhill and were drowned.

The Cottington Hill Witch legend relates to a village near Newbury, in Berkshire. There is a mysterious link here with the strange legends of Spring-heeled Jack, the leaping terror of Victorian London. On one of his wild exploits, Jack approached a sentry at Aldershot, one of the largest military training establishments in the United Kingdom. The soldier held his ground and warned Jack that he would shoot if Jack did not stop. For answer, Jack gave a wild peel of laughter and leaped over the sentry box. The guard fired at point blank range, but Jack raced on and leaped away quite unconcerned.

The Cottington Hill Witch caught bullets in her hands when her pursuers — some of Cromwell's finest Ironsides — fired at her repeatedly. Not to be beaten by man nor devil, one of the fearless Ironsides drew his sword and sliced her head open before shooting her at the base of the skull for good measure. That stopped her dead in her tracks! Her ghost — or a demonic evil entity in the form of the spectral witch — has allegedly been reported from the Cottington Hill area.

Another very strange Cottington Hill event took place when the 131-metre radio and television mast known as the Hannington Transmitter was taken over on Saturday November 26, 1977, at 5:10 p.m. A voice claiming to be an extraterrestrial named Vrillon, who said he was the commander of the Ashtar Galactic Command, superimposed itself over the ITN news and a cartoon that followed it. This strange broadcast lasted for approximately six minutes. Despite the best efforts of the police and investigators from the Independent Broadcasting Authority, the perpetrators were never caught.

The village of Welford in Berkshire had a magical post, known as Palmers' Post, which may once have referred to a point of pilgrimage (pilgrims were called Palmers). The local wizard, or wise man, used the post to entrap evil of every kind to prevent it from harming the villagers. When the motorway was built, the famous old post had to be removed to make way. There were a number of motorway accidents near the spot where the magical post had once stood, and villagers were convinced that when the workers had demolished the post they had inadvertently released the evil spirits and demons that were trapped there.

Hermitage Castle is situated in Hawick, in the area known as Lothian and Borders, in Britain. Throughout the early years of the fourteenth century, a singularly evil and unpleasant character named William de Soulis was Lord of Hermitage Castle and the surrounding area. He was a big, powerful man, and his muscular strength matched the evil power of his black magic and witchcraft. He is said to have kidnapped local children and used their blood for the dark magic that he practised in secret chambers deep inside the castle.

While performing his evil rituals, he was assisted by a horrifying familiar called Robin Redcap. Redcaps of this type were also called "dunters" or "powries." They have something in common with the evil dwarves and gnomes of mythology, or with corrupted elves and goblins. They are merciless, random killers, who murder innocent travellers to get the fresh blood they need to renew the stains on their red caps. Legend has it that if these red stains dry out, the redcap expires! As in all myths and legends, the evil entities have their specific vulnerabilities. Redcaps cannot bear to hear the Bible quoted at them. Each verse quoted causes one of their teeth to fall out.

De Soulis had little need of his murderous accomplice, however, because of his own massive size and strength and his knowledge of the infernal arts. His insatiable sexual appetites matched his mighty physique and he was in the habit of abducting attractive young women to satisfy his desires.

On one particular foray into the village, he abducted a young girl of the Armstrong Clan, whose father put up a valiant struggle to save her; but he was no match for de Soulis, who killed him on the spot. An angry crowd hemmed in de Soulis and, despite his enormous strength, they were about to kill him when Alexander Armstrong, Laird of Mangerton, arrived. Very surprisingly – and foolishly – he calmed his men down, insisted that de Soulis let go of the terrified girl, and then allowed him to leave in one piece. Such was de Soulis's evil nature that he could not accept that he had been rescued by a man he regarded as his inferior, so he invited Alexander to a feast in Hermitage – and promptly stabbed him in the back!

News of this outrage reached King Robert the Bruce – who exclaimed in fury "Boil Soulis!" The family of the murdered man took on the job with alacrity. They stormed the castle, and dragged de Soulis to the centre of Nine Stane Rig, an ancient henge in the vicinity of Hermitage. Here they used a great cauldron filled with boiling *lead* – no mere water for de Soulis the Sorcerer! Into this boiling metal their enemy was cast – and none of his evil magic or his redcap familiar could save him. His ghost, however, survives, in the form of an evil, demonic spectre which meets an equally evil black wizard in the dungeons of Hermitage Castle.

The Church of St. Peter and St. Paul in the village of West Clandon contains a wooden carving of a dragon. This was a particularly evil demonic creature that terrified the villagers and did great damage in the surrounding area. It was killed, according to the legend, by a soldier who was under sentence of death for desertion. He said that if the villagers would use their influence to obtain a pardon for him, he and his dog would take on the dragon. The promise of a pardon was obtained – dependent on his freeing the villagers from the terror of the demonic dragon. The battle took place, and the soldier won, largely because his loyal and valiant dog leaped on the dragon and took its attention long enough for the soldier to destroy it. The villagers were free, and their hero was pardoned.

Demonic dragon in the Church of St. Peter and St. Paul in West Clandon, Surrey, England.

The village of Frensham in Surrey has a mysterious witchcraft connection and large, authentic witch's cauldron. Mother Ludlam was a white witch, or wise woman, who lived in a cave not far from the Church of St. Mary the Virgin in Frensham. She was almost certainly a herbalist and healer. According to one legend, she was a kind and generous soul who would lend out utensils as the poor needed them. That was the best side of her nature — but there was another side to her, as well! When that evil side came to the top, she became furious, as if possessed.

One day, when a borrower failed to return the cauldron, Mother Ludlam flew into a rage and terrified the negligent borrower. Rather than face the witch's fury, the borrower raced to the church with the cauldron in the hope of escaping Mother Ludlam.

The second version of the legend says that the devil himself disapproved of her generosity and helpfulness and decided to put an end to it. He disguised himself as a poor villager and came to ask Mother Ludlam for the loan of her cauldron. She, however, recognized his cloven hoof-prints in the sand, and refused to lend it to him — so he promptly purloined it and tried to make his escape. Mother Ludlam went in hot pursuit. In order to try to escape from her, the devil took great leaps and bounds, and his landings and takeoffs created the sandstone hills near Frensham. These landmarks later became known as the Devil's Jumps. So anxious was Satan to get away from Mother Ludlam, that he dropped the cauldron — which was also known as a kettle in the middle ages — on the last of these sandstone hills. It, therefore, acquired the name of Kettlebury Hill. She found it, and took it to the Church of St. Mary the Virgin, where she knew that it would be perfectly safe from Satan.

There is yet a third version of the cauldron legend which states that at one time it could be borrowed from the fairies and elves who took care of it, if the would-be borrower climbed the hill called Stony Jump. The person had to whisper through a hole in the stone at the top to the little people who lived inside the hill. The cauldron would then be loaned. One careless borrower failed to return it, and the fairies put a spell on it so that it would follow her everywhere she went. This became so tiresome that, unable to bear it any longer, the careless borrower took it to the church at Frensham and collapsed there in front of the altar, begging God's forgiveness and protection. When she ventured to the door again, after resting in the church, the cauldron remained motionless.

The village of Shebbear lies between Holsworthy and Hatherleigh in Devon. Outside the village church, dedicated to St. Michael, lies a very large, heavy stone of an unusual material. There is a tradition in the village that each year, on November 5, the ringers from the church turn the stone over in order to keep the devil away. The legend explains that the stone came to be there when it dropped out of Satan's pocket as he fell from Heaven. *Could this mean that it was actually a meteorite?*

Witch's cauldron preserved in the Church of St. Mary the Virgin in Frensham.

Shebbear is mentioned frequently in the Domesday Book because the villagers always gave generously to support the crusades. That is all in keeping with the church's dedication to St. Michael, who is the warrior Archangel credited with overcoming Satan. It is noticeable that where a Christian church — like the tower of St. Michael at the top of Glastonbury Tor — is dedicated to Michael, there was usually an old pagan shrine where the church now stands: symbolically indicating Michael's triumph over Lucifer, and the Christian conquest of the "Old Religion."

A terrifying demonic phenomenon is reported by witnesses from the area of Devon known as Two Bridges, which is close to the village of Postbridge. Referred to as the Hairy Hands, this particularly unpleasant phenomenon has been blamed for a number of fatal road accidents in the area. A motorcyclist who was fortunate enough to survive the crash that they caused him, reported that he saw and felt two huge hairy disembodied hands over his own on the handlebars of his motorcycle. The hands steered his bike and caused him to crash.

On another occasion, caravanners were holidaying in the area. The husband was asleep, but his wife was fully awake. To her horror, she saw the huge hands crawling up the outside of their caravan window and approaching her sleeping husband. Realizing that they were something intensely evil and not of this world, she began to pray fervently that God and the holy angels would protect the man that she loved. Within a few seconds of saying her prayers, the hands seemed to shrink, lose their grip on the glass, and fall. There was no further sign of them.

Wicken Fen, in Cambridgeshire, is famous for reports of sightings of dark, shadowy, spectral, demonic hounds. These devil-dogs are reputed to have eyes the size of car headlamps and the legend warns passersby never to look directly into those glaring, orange-red orbs, because death will assuredly follow.

Where Spinney Abbey Farm is located in Wicken today, there was once an old priory, and witnesses claim that they can still hear the singing and chanting of the long-dead monks. Strange lights have been reported from across the Wicken Fen, and these are thought to be either natural gas causing will-o'-the-wisp effects, or strange demonic entities trying to lure the unwary into dangerous, boggy areas.

A remarkable report from Berry Well in Yorkshire records the presence of a mischievous demonic goose, which causes only minor problems and irritations rather than any serious evil. The well itself that gives Berry Well its name is situated in a wall not far from the Swinton Park Hotel, between the villages of High and Low Swinton.

Cresswell Crags, near the village of Cresswell, are on the border between Nottinghamshire and Derbyshire in England. There is a lake in the area and witnesses have reported a demonic form in the shape of a floating head that emerges from the water and is then seen in the shape of a witch. This demonic spectre moves toward a limestone cave and then vanishes into it. One of the caves in the area is called Mother Grundy's Parlour, and was occupied for thousands of years in prehistoric times. Was the witch whose phantom now appears in the lake once a woman named Grundy? Artefacts found in the caves have included bone carved with a horse's head, which may well have been used for black magic in the remote past.

The village of Flixton in North Yorkshire is close to Scarborough, and an interesting local feature is the area known as Flixton Carr. In Mesolithic times this was submerged below neighbouring Lake Pickering, but gradually became fenland before assuming its current form. There are reports of a demonic entity in the Flixton area that assumes the shape of a huge werewolf with the traditional glowing red eyes.

Horbury, Wakefield, Yorkshire, is the site of reports of a hideous demonic creature, known in that area as a "boggart." Two witnesses actually reported being attacked by it. They described the thing as being ice-cold to the touch, covered in hair, and having eyes that glowed in an abnormal way.

Kirkby Malham, near Skipton in Yorkshire, has a church dedicated to St. Michael the Archangel, which is often an indicator that evil has been overcome there at some time in the past. According to the traditional legend, Satan sets out a meal once a year in the Kirkby Malham churchyard in order to lure the unwary down to hell. On one occasion, it is said that the fearless local parish priest accepted the invitation in order to prevent any of his parishioners from being tempted. He drove Satan and the demons away from their infernal repast by asking for salt. Salt is regarded as sacred and is frequently used in exorcisms. Lucifer and his acolytes decided not to linger to find out what the priest was planning to do to them with the salt!

One of the few reports of an assault by an incubus comes from Stockton-on-Tees in North Yorkshire. The witness was a nineteen-year-old girl living at home with her parents. She awoke in the middle of the night to find the demonic entity with its hand on her leg. She screamed in terror and her parents raced into her room to help her. The entity then vanished. The family requested an exorcism, which was duly carried out, and no further problems were reported.

During the years of the witch hunts, several witches were executed in Gloucestershire and buried at crossroads in the traditional manner. One such crossroads near Poulton, not far from Cirencester, is still referred to as Betty's Grave, after a witch named Betty who was executed and buried there. Numerous witnesses have reported seeing her demonic wraith floating around the crossroads.

Our final example comes from Leckhampton Hill, near Cheltenham in Gloucestershire, where an outcrop of limestone has ancient legends attached to it maintaining that it is a gateway to hell, and that the unwary can be drawn down it by Satan to the infernal regions.

The Church of Satan and Other Satanic Groups

The Church of Satan uses as its logo what its members refer to as "The Sigil of Baphomet." This design shows a demonic goat-like head inside a five-pointed star inside an annulus — with mysterious magical letters between the two circles. The author and magician Alphonse Louis Constant (1810-75) called himself Eliphas Lévi in an attempt to transform his French name into Hebrew, although he was not Jewish. He said that the pentagram, also known as the blazing star, symbolized vast intellectual ability and autocracy.

He said that the sigil indicated order versus chaos; the lamb versus the goat; Lucifer against Vesper (the morning and evening stars); Holy Mary against the demoness Lilith. It also stands for victory versus death and symbolizes darkness opposed to light.

Most of the grimoires associate the pentagram with King Solomon's seal and the power it gave him to control and imprison demons. The French occultist Stanislas de Guaita (1861-97) was an enthusiastic Rosicrucian and an expert on mysticism, magic, and esotericism. He was enthusiastic about Eliphas Lévi's work and hailed him as one of the greatest geniuses of the nineteenth century. Guaita's book *La Clef de la Magie Noire* (The Key to Black Magic) was published in 1897, and contained a picture of the traditional demon-goat face inside the five-pointed star.

Lévi refers to Lilith and Sammael in his writings and illustrations, and some versions of the mysterious sigil include their names. Lévi does not, however, refer to Leviathan in his writings and drawings, whereas Guaita does, and writes it in its Hebrew form in association with the sigil.

The symbolic goat head is thought to go all the way back to ancient Egypt, where it is referred to as "The Goat of Mendes" and is associated with an entity called Neter Amon, meaning "the one who is hidden." The two circles enclosing the star are thought to represent the Ophites, also called the Serpentinians, who flourished in Syria and Egypt toward the

One possible origin of the Sigil.

end of the first century A.D. They worshipped the serpent referred to in the Eden narrative in Genesis, and treated it as the symbol of knowledge. As this serpent was also felt to represent Satan or Lucifer, its relevance for Satanists becomes clear.

Writer, occultist, and musician Anton Szandor LaVey (1930-1997), originally Howard Stanton Levey, became the founder and High Priest of the Church of Satan. His main life principles were materialism, secularism, individualism, freedom, and independence.

Growing up, Levey's father, Michael Joseph Levey, worked as a liquor distributor. He was second-generation American-French from Omaha.

Howard's mother was Gertrude Augusta Coultron. She was the daughter of a Ukrainian mother and a Russian father, who had both become American citizens in 1900.

Young Anton grew up in the San Francisco Bay area, where his parents encouraged his musical interests, especially with the steam-organ, known as the calliope. He was also a skilled instrumentalist on the pipe-organ. Anton left school as soon as he could and worked in a circus and various nightclubs, as well as a few burlesque theatres. His cynicism toward orthodox religion waned when he noticed that some men who regarded themselves as pillars of the church also regularly attended the raunchy burlesque shows.

Anton married Carole Lansing in 1950 and they had a daughter, Karla LaVey. They divorced in 1960 and Anton formed a relationship with Diane Hegarty, who became the mother of his second daughter, Zeena Galatea LaVey.

Those who knew and understood Anton best felt that he never deliberately set out to create a new religion or a new philosophical and theological approach to life — yet that seems to be more or less what he accomplished with his Church of Satan. LaVey thought that he could discern a real need for something that would oppose what he regarded as the stagnation of traditional, orthodox Christianity as embodied in the church. In his view, Christianity was an obstacle to all social progress and scientific advancement.

He felt that he couldn't accomplish these desired changes by himself. One human being was too small. It needed someone bigger and altogether stronger than he was. He wanted a figurehead for what he saw as a quest for real justice in an unjust world. He wanted to gain help from someone — or some*thing* — that understood human weaknesses, human indiscretions, and human desires. In LaVey's analysis of human history and human progress, people who had rebelled against God — as the church misrepresented him — were the very people who had made the most important scientific discoveries, and brought about the greatest improvements in human society.

LaVey wanted a leader who would rebel against conventional society. He wanted a leader who was a genuine revolutionary, who would appeal to the irrepressible, imaginative, creative part of human nature in ways that the church did not. Early on in his quest for such a great leader, he came to the conclusion that there was only one who would fit the profile: Satan. It seemed to Anton, from his readings of history and from his introspective research into his own human nature, that Satan was the leader for him. He saw Satan as the being who tempted human beings with offers of delightful things that were there for the taking — if only human beings had the courage to defy convention and reach for them.

LaVey saw Satan as the provider of power and the holder of the key to the cosmic secrets. Anton argued that instead of listing sins and taboos to frighten humanity into a kind of guilty subservience, Satan was the leader who advocated the wildest human indulgence as the surest road to happiness and satisfaction. In LaVey's mind, Satan was the only one who truly understood humanity — and was, therefore, the best possible leader.

From the 1950s onward, LaVey established a reputation as a black magician, and others who shared some of his ideas began to gather around him. One of his interests at this time was demonic geometry, and his followers took to wearing oddly shaped black and red identifying badges. The group became known as the Order of the Trapezoid.

Readers in Australia and Britain would tend to use the geometrical term *trapezium* instead of the American usage of *trapezoid*. Either word indicates a four-sided figure with one pair of parallel sides. The normal, traditional version in maths textbooks is to show the top shorter than the base, but parallel to it — so that it looks rather like the cross-section of a podium on which a speaker can stand to address the audience. This trapezoid badge was decorated with the picture of a demon whose bat-like wings were outstretched.

Members of LaVey's Order of the Trapezoid included European aristocrats, lawyers, doctors of medicine, filmmakers, authors, police officers, property owners, anthropologists, deep-sea divers, manufacturers, business people, and merchants of all types. They were a very remarkable, powerful, and wealthy cross-section.

LaVey, at the centre of his assortment of like-minded followers, was dedicated to newness and difference. He did not want a mere set of religious rules, theories, or doctrines that his adherents would be expected to follow. He hated the hypocrisy that he thought he saw in much traditional religion. He detested the taboos and restrictions that went with orthodox religion. He felt that those religious rules and regulations led to social ignorance and were serious obstacles to any hope of radical social development.

If people were freed from religious laws, he argued, they would be able to apply and enjoy the black magic spells, charms, and formulas that he and his associates gloried in. It is important to analyze what LaVey himself thought about black magic at this point in the development of his Order. He felt as if he and his followers were really learning about ways to control events in the environment, events that could not be controlled using traditional, orthodox methods.

What if there are serious grains of truth in his theories about magic? What if, by using what LaVey regarded as magic, he and his followers were actually creating portals to the enormous potential power concealed – and largely neglected – in the depths of the human mind? What if *belief* in the black magic charms, the talismans, the spells, and incantations that the Order of the Trapezoid used opened doorways in the mind that were normally tightly closed and camouflaged?

The placebo effect is well-known in medical research. The patient swallowing harmless medicines made from innocent sugar and fruit juices can often defeat an illness because he *believes* that the placebo he has been given is a potent, newly developed therapy – the pinnacle of modern pharmaceutical technology. Be that as it may, LaVey and his followers were convinced that black magic – as they defined it – really could produce effects that orthodox science could not.

Anton and his followers refined their magical arts until they felt that they *were* achieving their required results by directing their wills and their magic into areas where they wanted to make favourable changes. And they believed that their magic was making those changes happen: careers were advanced; attractive sex partners were acquired; money poured in; dangerous rivals and outright enemies were removed. It was an almost inescapable conclusion for members of the Order of the Trapezoid that under Anton's guidance and leadership they really had made contact with some strange Dark Force in Nature, and were now wielding whatever that force was to their own great advantage.

For Anton and his friends and colleagues in the Order of the Trapezoid, the time had come to reach the next stage. They felt that they had acquired something real, rational, and down to earth. Their system recognized and lived happily enough with humanity's basest instincts – however selfish, carnal, and lustful those instincts might be. There was no question of feeling guilty – or of trying to impose guilt on others. The whole idea of sin to them was something artificial, something manufactured by the church. They were immune to it!

LaVey decided that the new organization he was planning to create had to be bigger than his Order of the Trapezoid. They would be its nucleus. They would be its leaders. But the new organization would have to be an actual church – the Church of Satan – then it would be big enough to challenge the old moral and ethical religions like Christianity and, hopefully, from LaVey's point of view, blast them to hell! He knew well enough that there had been secretive Satanist underground movements for millennia – but now for the very first time in history they were daring to come out into the open as an officially organized and recognized religion.

LaVey decided to found his Church of Satan on Walpurgisnacht, the Spring Equinox, on the night of April 30/May 1. The year 1966 was to become the First Year of the Reign of Satan. As part of the preparation for its inauguration, LaVey shaved his head – rather like the old circus strongmen he had known from the days of his youth.

Less than two years after its inauguration, LaVey's Church of Satan was achieving worldwide publicity. Two of his well-known members – socialite Judith Case and journalist John Raymond – had had a satanic wedding. The nude female altar had attracted the paparazzi, and their pictures had featured in a great many magazines.

A number of LaVey's early Church of Satan rituals were simply Black Masses – blasphemous inversions of the Christian Eucharist. Then he started to develop what he referred to as "the untapped grey area between religion and psychiatry." He felt, as he had done in the early days of the Order of the Trapezoid, that mental energy, perhaps even bio-electrical brain energy, could be harvested and *directed* at their services. He believed that real black magic existed, that it had genuine power, and that it could be used to affect the environment in ways that favoured him and the members of his church.

The next step was to arrange a satanic baptism for his angelic-looking three-year-old daughter, Zeena. He made a statement to the effect that instead of cleansing her from original sin, the satanic baptism would "glorify her natural instincts and intensify her lust for life."

The words of this satanic baptism service concluded with: "And so we dedicate your life to love, to passion, to indulgence, and to Satan, and the way of darkness. Hail Zeena! Hail Satan!"

Having had a satanic wedding and a satanic baptism, only a satanic funeral was needed to complete the Church of Satan's major ritual provision. The opportunity arose when Edward Olsen, a naval man, was killed in a road accident in San Francisco. He and his attractive young wife, Pat, had both been enthusiastic members of the Church of Satan, and it was she who asked the naval authorities for their support for Edward's satanic funeral. A naval guard of honour was present, and a salute was fired. The naval servicemen stood smartly to attention alongside the black-robed Church of Satan members.

It was said in some circles that beautiful film star Jayne Mansfield's traumatic death in a horrendous 1967 car accident when she was only thirty-four years old was linked with the Church of Satan. Some accounts alleged that LaVey had placed a demonic curse on her boyfriend, lawyer Sam Brody, because Brody had criticized him. Brody was killed in the car alongside Jayne. Other accounts allege that LaVey inadvertently cut through the *Bild-Zeitung* magazine picture of Jayne – removing her head – while he was clipping out a piece about the Church of Satan from the other side of the magazine page.

LaVey actually played the role of Satan in the 1968 film *Rosemary's Baby*. The film was a powerful recruiting mechanism for his Church of Satan.

Anton died on October 29, 1997, leaving his administrative colleagues to carry on running the Church of Satan, which is still functioning effectively today from its headquarters in New York. A group known as The First Satanic Church was started on October 31, 1999, under the guidance of Karla LaVey, Anton's eldest daughter. The church, of which Karla is the High Priestess, is headquartered in San Francisco.

Luciferians venerate Lucifer as a light-bringer, and see their organization as being similar to, but not identical with, Satanism. To them, following

Lucifer as a light source is a more positive and relaxed form of worship and general conduct than actually being Satanists.

A group of Ophite Satanists refer to themselves as the Coven of our Lady of Endor, a reference to the Witch of Endor in the bible (first book of Samuel 28:3-25). The cult was founded in 1948 by Herbert Arthur Sloane in Toledo, Ohio. They are largely a Gnostic group who venerate Satan in the form of the serpent in Eden, whom they regard as the wise one who gave knowledge to Eve.

Another group are known as the Temple of Set. They claim to be the world's leading religious organization that sends its devotees along the so-called "left-hand path." It was founded in 1975 by Michael Aquino and a few members of LaVey's Church of Satan who disagreed with the way it was being run. The members of the Temple of Set make what they call "enlightened individualism" their principal aim. They set out to improve themselves by academic learning, by practical trial and error, and by a series of initiation processes into higher and higher mysteries. They worship the old Egyptian god Set, or Seth, whom they conceive of as the dark, secret power behind the Hebrew idea of Satan as an adversary.

The Order of Nine Angles, also referred to as ONA, was originally founded in Britain in the 1960s. It is alleged to have politically ultra-right-wing fascist leanings, and is organized around small, secret cells of members. These cells are called nexions. Three groups – the Camlad, the Noctulians, and the Temple of the Sun – came together to form ONA. There are thought to be groups of the ONA in Canada, the United States, Russia, Iceland, Australia, and Europe.

There are numerous other contemporary Satanist groups – both theistic and atheistic in nature – that can easily be studied via their websites.

Does Satan Exist?

Research and analysis into Satanism and demonology is not like abstract theological or philosophical speculation — useful as both of them are. Research into Satanism and demonology asks serious, pragmatic, and realistic questions about the objective existence — or otherwise — of the paranormal beings described as devils and demons. Are they there or not? And if they are there, what are they like? How might they affect us? And what can we do about them?

The great Abrahamic religions — Judaism, Christianity, and Islam — all traditionally acknowledge the existence of Satan, Lucifer, or Iblis, although there are significant differences in the way that these three faiths regard him. Is he merely an honest, obedient and loyal servant of God, using his adversarial powers, as outlined in the book of Job, to tempt human beings, to see whether we are able to withstand his lures and blandishments? Is he part of the divine plan to ensure that we are using our free will and our decision-making powers correctly, to choose good rather than evil for ourselves?

What if he is *not* obeying God, but rather has rebelled against God, and has turned all his hatred, venom, and spite on the human race, which God has made and loves? Is it like the old music-hall joke from the days of horse-drawn deliveries, "He couldn't fight the milkman — so he kicked the milkman's horse"? Is Satan a fallen angel, hopelessly inferior in power and strength to archangels such as Michael the Warrior — and so far below God in power that they are barely comparable at all? If he has no chance at all against God or the mighty archangels who do God's bidding, does he spitefully kick us — the milkman's horse? This raises a huge question about ethics, morality, and justice. If it is the duty of the strong to protect the weak and care for them, why does the Divine Milkman *allow* Satan to kick his horse? Theodicy — the area of theology that tries to explain the cosmic problem of a good God in a world of human suffering — is a very difficult and complex area. It is an intellectual minefield.

Some kind of answer is forthcoming if we begin with the premise that love is the most desirable component of the entire universe, and that God's own perfect nature is love personified. Love cannot exist unless we have genuine free will. It cannot be bought. It cannot be coerced through fear. It can only be given freely and willingly. If the greatest joy that Heaven can offer is to live in true and deep loving relationships with God and with one another *forever*, then free will is a prerequisite of that exquisite eternal joy. If genuine free will exists — and we are convinced that it does — then there must exist alongside it the horrendous possibility of evil in all its forms: murder, theft, cruelty, selfishness....

What about the question of relative power in a being that has free will? An evil maggot cannot do much. An evil mouse or bird can do relatively much more than a maggot — but very little compared to bigger, stronger animals. An evil cat or dog can be a real problem. Human beings vary in size and strength. A Third Dan martial artist such as co-author Lionel can put his fist through a door panel or kill an opponent with one blow. That kind of lethal fighting power should never be used for evil. A lion, tiger, or elephant that chooses evil can potentially do tremendous damage and cause great suffering. An evil being with access to a knife, a gun, a bomb, poison gas, or toxic bacteria can do far worse damage than a rogue elephant. What if such an ill-intentioned human being has access to nuclear weapons? What if an evil extraterrestrial alien has access to laser weapons or death-rays far beyond our earthly weapon technology? The more powerful you are, the more damage you can inflict should you choose to employ your power for evil purposes. What kind of super-human powers might an angel have — even a fallen angel — if angels exist?

If we can imagine that Satan, or Lucifer, really was an angel who made a wrong moral choice, how much harm can such a being do? How much suffering can he cause?

If God or one of the Archangels intervenes to destroy the evil fallen angel, or to take all his powers away from him, *what has happened to genuine free will?* Theodicy is indeed a difficult academic jungle through which theologians and philosophers must try to cut their way. It is complicated

How many innocent women suffered because of the witch hunt?

further by the vast problem of consistency throughout the universe: the laws of energy and matter that seem never to alter.

That consistency of behaviour for matter and energy makes sense, of course. If red was green when it felt like it, if hot could change to cold at a whim, if hard and soft surfaces changed like the weather, if love and hatred rotated uncertainly like a top spinning on cobblestones, then we should never be able to understand the universe at all – and we know little enough of its mysteries now when most things do seem to be consistent.

Does the consistency hypothesis help with theodicy? Suppose that it is part of God's plan and design that matter and energy should behave consistently throughout space and time in his universe – then when evil is done using matter and energy, the physical effects will be exactly the same as they are when a good person uses matter and energy to heal the sick, to feed the hungry, or to house the homeless. A loving, caring doctor can use a hypodermic needle to save a patient by injecting antibiotic. An evil drug dealer can use the same piece of equipment to enslave an addict. The laws of physics behind the injection work in exactly the same way in both cases.

It can be argued that it is never any part of the will or intention of a loving God for helpless people to drown in a flood, to be crushed when an earthquake brings down buildings, or to die in a fast-moving forest fire. The flood, the earthquake, and the fire all behave consistently according to the laws of physics. If they didn't, brave and ingenious men and women would not be able to learn how to protect the vulnerable when disaster strikes. So when we ask why helpless and innocent people suffer in such disasters, we need to ask *why* they were living in hazardous places: in areas that flood, on earthquake belts, on the fertile slopes below a smouldering volcano. Were they perhaps ignorant of the potential hazards of the area? If someone who was better informed, some powerful leader, or some ruling politician, had chosen to do something to help, or persuade, those vulnerable people, *their suffering and death might not have happened.*

So if an aggrieved Satan exists as an evil being seeking to harm us all, the essential consistency of the laws of nature works just as effectively for him as it does for an angel of mercy alleviating human pain and grief.

Who is Satan? What sort of being is he, and what are his motives? He may exist in personal form, he may not. In what other forms might he exist?

Suppose that evil is not personified in a malicious and malevolent fallen angel like Satan: then where does it come from? Perhaps it is all in the depths of the human mind, after all. The noblest and kindest men and women can still be capable of dark thoughts occasionally. The ignoble and unkind savour their dark thoughts most of the time! If evil is not embodied in the person of Satan, might it not be lurking within all of us? Selfishness, greed, and ruthless, unfettered ambition can lead even the best men and women to think, speak, and do evil. If that is the real solution to the problem of Satan's existence — and it may well be so — then he may be regarded as a subordinate personality living inside every human being. Some really good characters keep him tightly chained and restrained. Most of us let him out now and then when we are seriously provoked. A few really selfish and evil types let him lead them around as if they were helpless dogs that belonged to him! Evil is in command — the human personality of such people has become subordinate to their evil impulses.

In the course of this research and analysis we have considered many possibilities for the existence and nature of Satan and the demons. It is difficult if not impossible to reach a definitive conclusion. On balance, evil seems more likely to be an unwelcome product of the human mind than to be an entity in its own right — but it can't be proved absolutely in either direction.

What matters most is how we deal with it. Whether we are fighting evil entities, or evil thoughts that we ourselves have created, goodness can conquer it. An effort of will can hold evil in check. When we make that effort of will, we are moving toward the light and away from the darkness. It is an effort that is well worth making.

BIBLIOGRAPHY

Anonymous. *Hamel, the Obeah Man.* Jamaica: Macmillan Caribbean Publishing, 2008.

Blavatsky, H.P. Articles from her *Lucifer: A Theosophical Magazine* (1887–91) reprinted in *The Dennis Wheatley Library of the Occult.* London: Sphere Books Ltd., 1974.

Brookesmith, Peter, ed. *Cult and* Occult. London: Guild Publishing, 1985.

Carey, Margret. *Myths and Legends of Africa.* London: Hamlyn, 1970.

Carroll, Latrobe. *Death and its Mysteries.* London: T. Fisher Unwin Ltd., 1923.

Clayton, Peter A. *Chronicle of the Pharaohs.* London: Thames and Hudson Ltd., 1994.

Cottrell, L. *The Lost Pharaohs.* London: Pan Books Ltd., 1960.

David-Neel, Alexandra. *Initiations and Initiates in Tibet.* New York: University Books, 1959.

_____. *The Secret Oral Traditions in Tibetan Sects.* San Francisco: City Lights Publishing, 1964.

_____. *With Mystics and Magicians in Tibet.* New York: Dover Publications, 1971.

Dodson, Aidan. *Monarchs of the Nile.* London: Rubicon Press, 1995.

Encyclopaedia Britannica: Britannica Online: Miscellaneous references as required. www.eb.com, 2008.

Fairley, John, & Welfare, Simon. *Arthur C Clarke's World of Strange Powers.* London: W. Collins Sons & Co Ltd., 1985.

Fanthorpe, Patricia and Lionel. *The Holy Grail Revealed.* Southern California: Newcastle Publishing Co. Inc., 1982.

_____. *Secrets of Rennes le Château.* York Beach, ME: Samuel Weiser Inc., 1992.

_____. *The Oak Island Mystery.* Toronto: Hounslow Press, 1995.

_____. *The World's Greatest Unsolved Mysteries*. Toronto: Hounslow Press, 1997.

_____. *The World's Most Mysterious People*. Toronto: Hounslow Press, 1998.

_____. *The World's Most Mysterious Places*. Toronto: Hounslow Press. 1999.

_____. *Mysteries of the Bible*. Toronto: Hounslow Press, 1999.

_____. *Death the Final Mystery*. Toronto: Hounslow Press, 2000.

_____. *The World's Most Mysterious Objects*. Toronto: Hounslow Press, 2002.

_____. *The World's Most Mysterious Murders*. Toronto: Hounslow Press, 2003.

_____. *Unsolved Mysteries of the Sea*. Toronto: Hounslow Press, 2004.

_____. *Mysteries of Templar Treasure and the Holy Grail*. York Beach, ME: Samuel Weiser Inc., 2004.

_____. *The World's Most Mysterious Castles*. Toronto: Hounslow Press, 2005.

_____. *Mysteries and Secrets of the Templars: The Story Behind the Da Vinci Code*. Toronto: Hounslow Press, 2005.

_____. *Mysteries and Secrets of the Masons*. Toronto: Hounslow Press, 2006.

_____. *Mysteries and Secrets of Time*. Toronto: Hounslow Press, 2007.

_____. *Mysteries and Secrets of Voodoo*. Toronto: Dundurn Press, 2008.

_____. *Secrets of the World's Undiscovered Treasures*. Toronto: Dundurn Press, 2009.

Faraone, Christopher A. "Binding and Burying the Forces of Evil: The Defensive Use of 'Voodoo Dolls' in Ancient Greece." California: *Classical Antiquity Magazine*, Vol. 10, No. 2, 1991.

Frazer, James George Sir. *The Golden Bough*. New York: The Macmillan Co., 1922.

Gettings, Fred. *Encyclopedia of the Occult*. London: Guild Publishing, 1986.

_____. *Secret Symbolism in Occult Art*. New York: Harmony Books, 1987.

Graves, Robert (Introduction). *Larousse Encyclopaedia of Mythology*. London: Paul Hamlyn, 1959.

Grimal, Nicolas. *A History of Ancient Egypt*. Oxford: Blackwell, 1988.

Guerber, H.A. *Myths and Legends of the Middle Ages*. London: Studio Editions Ltd., 1994.

Haining, P. *Witchcraft and Black Magic*. London: The Hamlyn Publishing Group Ltd., 1971.

Harrison, Michael. *The Roots of Witchcraft*. London: Tandem, 1975.

Hougham, Paul. *The Atlas of Mind, Body and Spirit*. London: Octopus Publishing Group, 2006.

King, R.C. *Dragons*. London: Penguin Books Ltd., 1979.
Lewis, V. *Satan's Mistress*. Shepperton, Middlesex, UK: Nauticalia Ltd., 1997.
Lloyd, Gwynedd, ed. *Lotions and Potions*. London: National Federation of Women's Institutes, 1968.
MacCall, A. *The Medieval Underworld*. New York: Barnes and Noble, 1979.
Martin, Lois. *The History of Witchcraft*. Harpenden, UK: Pocket Essentials, 2007.
Newton, Toyne. *The Dark Worship*. London: Vega, 2002.
Ogden, Daniel. *Magic, Witchcraft and Ghosts in the Greek and Roman World: A Sourcebook*. Oxford: Oxford University Press, 2002.
Playfair, Guy Lyon. *The Unknown Power*. St. Albans, Hertfordshire, UK: Granada Publishing Ltd., 1977.
Reeves, Nicholas, and Richard H. Wilkinson. *Complete Valley of the Kings (Tombs & Treasures of Egypt's Greatest Pharaohs)*. London: Thames & Hudson Ltd., 1966.
Schwartz, Gary E. R., and Linda G.S. Russek. *The Living Energy Universe*. Charlottesville, VA: Hampton Roads Publishing, 1999.
Sharper Knowlson, T. *The Origins of Popular Superstitions and Customs*. London: Studio Editions Ltd., 1995.
Shaw, Ian. *The Oxford History of Ancient Egypt*. Oxford: Oxford University Press, 2000.
Singer, Marian. *Everything You Need To Know About Witchcraft*. Newton Abbot, UK: David and Charles, 2005.
Spence, Lewis. *Ancient Egyptian Myths and Legends*. New York: Dover Publications Inc., 1990.
_____. *The Encyclopedia of the Occult*. London: Bracken Books, 1988.
St. Clair, David. *Drum and Candle*. New York: Bell Publishing, 1971.
Tucker, R. *Strange Gospels*. London: HarperCollins, 1989.

Also by Lionel and Patricia Fanthorpe

The Big Book of Mysteries
978-1-55488-779-8 $19.99

From Atlantis to Nostradamus, Masons to Templars, Lionel and Patricia Fanthorpe have explored some of the greatest mysteries ever known in this world and beyond. Secret societies, lost treasures, and legendary monsters — all have been carefully researched, many investigated in person, and now presented with illustrations and photographs in one super-sized collection to satisfy everyone's curiosity. If you've ever felt the burning desire to know more about life's great mysteries, then *The Big Book of Mysteries* is for you — no element of the unknown is safe from the Fanthorpes' scrutinizing eyes.

Mysteries and Secrets of Voodoo
978-1-55002-784-6 $24.99

The secrets of Santeria, Voodoo, and Obeah are among the oldest enigmas in the world. Their roots go back to pre-historic Africa — perhaps beyond. From the sixteenth century onward, the slave trade brought these ancient mysteries to the West, where they blended strangely with traditional Christianity. This integration of the two faiths slowly evolved to form the many varieties of Santeria, Obeah, and Voudoun that are widely practised throughout the world today. Lionel and Patricia explore the customs, history, and mystery of these religions to find out what powers these old religions still possess.

Available at your favourite bookseller.

What did you think of this book?
Visit *www.dundurn.com* for reviews, videos, updates, and more!

www.ingramcontent.com/pod-product-compliance
Lightning Source LLC
Chambersburg PA
CBHW070644160426
43194CB00009B/1574